My Sheep Hear My Voice

Hearing
God's Voice
in Everyday Life

By Bonnie Wester Connolly

My Sheep Hear My Voice: Hearing God's Voice in Everyday Life
Copyright © 2020 by Bonnie W. Connolly

Published by TrueNorth Publishing
10380 Boundary Creek Terrace N., Maple Grove, MN 55369
www.truenorthpublishingdt.com
Manufactured by Snowfall Press, Monument, CO 80132

Cover design and layout: Cheryl Barr

Unless otherwise noted Scripture quotations are from THE HOLY
BIBLE, NEW INTERNATIONAL VERSION®, NIV® Copyright © 1973,
1978, 1984, 2011 by Biblica, Inc.™ Used by permission. All rights reserved worldwide.
Scriptures marked AMP are taken from the AMPLIFIED BIBLE (AMP):
Scripture taken from the AMPLIFIED ® BIBLE, Copyright © 1954, 1958,
1962, 1964, 1965, 1987 by The Lockman Foundation. Used by permission
(www.Lockman.org).
Scriptures marked KJV are taken from the KING JAMES VERSION
(KJV): KING JAMES VERSION, public domain.
Scripture marked TLB are taken from THE LIVING BIBLE (TLB): Scripture taken from THE LIVING BIBLE copyright© 1971. Used by permission of Tyndale House Publishers, Inc., Carol Stream, Illinois 60188. All
rights reserved.

ISBN: 978-0-9970752-4-3

Published in the United States of America

DEDICATION

This book is dedicated to my Lord and Savior, Jesus Christ for teaching me to hear His voice. I also dedicate this book to my family, friends, and future generations. May they all learn to hear God's voice in their everyday lives.

ACKNOWLEDGMENTS

I sincerely thank the following people who have encouraged me during the writing of this book:

- *Delores Topliff. Editor, Adjunct Instructor at the University of Northwestern, St. Paul, MN, and dear friend, who taught me many principles of grammar and sentence structure, as well as much about writing and publishing a book.*

- *Cheryl Barr. Without you, this book may not have a cover picture, and may not be formatted. Thank you for praying and encouraging me throughout this writing journey.*

- *Judy Comstock. Thank you for editing. Your English teacher skills were incredibly helpful.*

- *My husband, Mike. Thank you for your love, encouragement, and support throughout our forty years of marriage. Your suggestions were valuable.*

- *Our adult children, Krista and Brian. Thank you for your love, encouragement, and editing skills.*

- *Relatives and friends who prayed and helped me fine tune my writing.*

"My sheep hear My voice, and I
know them, and they follow Me."
(John 10:27 KJV)

FOREWORD

Bonnie Connolly is an American wife, mother, grand-mother of twins, Adult Nurse Practitioner, and lover of God. From her early twenties on, her growing desire to know God deeply drove her spiritual journey forward. Through good and difficult times, that search remains her underlying life theme. God led her into a professional nursing career and joined her to Mike in Christian mar-riage, but those successes didn't guarantee that life would be easy. Sometimes we get to know our Lord best as He sustains us through the challenging times when we dis-cover we cannot continue without a closer relationship with Him.

One of Bonnie's greatest strengths is that she faithfully journaled in all seasons. Another is that she draws near to her Savior through skilled piano playing in her home as well as supporting many church choirs and programs. She loves to sing, writing down the songs she receives from her Savior to sing back to Him, as well as sharing with others.

This book records the journey of her up and down times while also moving steadily forward. It honestly shares her tests and doubts but ends with victories gained in the process which become tools for the future.

Bonnie writes her story and its hard-won lessons in the hope it will provide strength and insights to those reading this personal and intimate, faith-filled book. I believe you will find wisdom and encouragement inside.

-Delores Topliff

INTRODUCTION

In John 10:27, Jesus said, "My sheep hear My voice and I know them and they follow me..." (KJV). This verse implies that Jesus' followers hear His voice. I am a follower of Jesus and hear His voice today. As one of His sheep, I talk with Him, and He talks with me. I don't hear an audible voice, yet deep within my spirit, I sense impressions of what He is saying.

Who do I refer to as He? When I use "He" I mean God, Jesus the Lord, and His Spirit. I believe that God the Father, Jesus, and His Spirit are One. God is the Creator of everything and everyone. Jesus lived on this earth, and after His resurrection, He sent His Holy Spirit to live in us by invitation.

So, how do I know that I hear God's voice when several voices in my mind clamor for attention? How do I know whether my thoughts originate from God, Satan, or my own thoughts? Over the years, I have come to discern some differences.

God's thoughts are spontaneous, gentle, healing and loving. They encourage, edify, exhort, comfort, and sometimes speak of the future. God's voice reflects His nature as described in Scripture. His thoughts inspire excitement, faith, life, and peace in my soul.

Satan's words bring guilt, condemnation, and despair. They kill, steal, and destroy—even to influence us to harm or destroy ourselves.

In the 1980's, as Christians growing in our faith, my husband and I were part of a local non-denominational church, where people had a hunger for a deeper fellowship with God. We used one of the spiritual gifts to give prophetic messages to individuals or the church. I longed to have a prophet speak words of prophecy over me. A prophecy is a Spirit-prompted message from God to an individual or church to strengthen, encourage, and comfort (1 Corinthians 14:3).

To prophesy is to give a message to an individual or congregation, which provides insight, predict future events, or give warning, correction, edification, strengthening, and comfort.

During this time, I had a conversation with a friend about how God speaks to us in many ways, not only when a modern day prophet speaks to us in the manner we often experienced in our church. She brought up Hebrews 1:1-2, which says, "In the past, God spoke to our forefathers through the prophets at many times and in various ways, but in these last days He has spoken to us by His Son, whom He appointed heir of all things, and through whom He made the universe." It was a short conversation, yet I remember the profound effect it had on me. I realized that I relied more on others, especially prophets in our church, than on allowing God to speak directly to me.

Years later, my husband, and I moved to a different city and a new church. Prophetic words, especially to individuals, were seldom given. I had a spiritual desire to hear from God and wondered when and how He would speak to me.

I searched the Scriptures that describe instances when God spoke to His people. The Bible is full of such conversations. Here are some examples:

In Genesis 3:8-10, the Lord God called to Adam and asked, "Where are you?"

He answered, "I heard you in the garden and I was afraid because I was naked so I hid."

In Exodus 3:4, God called to him from within the burning bush, "Moses! Moses!"

And Moses said, "Here I am."

In 1 Samuel 3:3-18, God called Samuel's name three times but Samuel thought that Eli had called him. When

Eli recognized that it was God calling the boy, Eli told Samuel to say, "Speak, for your servant is listening." Then, God spoke to Samuel, a mere child, and Samuel heard Him.

The Major and Minor Prophets in the Bible heard God's voice. God said to Jeremiah, "You will seek me and find me when you seek me with all your heart" (Jeremiah 29:13). I was definitely at that point of seeking God.

Some of my favorite old hymns speak about hearing Jesus' voice. In the hymn, "He Lives" the author Alfred H. Ackley wrote, "… And He walks with me and talks with me along life's narrow way." In another, "In the Garden," C. Austin Miles wrote the words, "And He walks with me, and He talks with me, and He tells me I am His own." These hymn writers assert that Jesus talks with them. Is that so unusual? I don't think so.

God speaks to us in many ways. One way is when I take my Bible, journal, and pen and sit in a quiet room. I become still, quiet my mind, and read scripture, devotional books, or sing praise and worship songs. I may ask God how He views my situation, a person in my life, or how He views me. I share my sorrows and joys. If I sense God's thoughts in my mind, I record these conversations in my journal. Do I experience these conversations every day? No, because sometimes God is silent or I don't take the time to listen.

Through the years, I have written entries in over a hundred journals. In 1991, the Holy Spirit led me to compile these conversations with Him into a book so that I would remember His words. God spoke to Jeremiah in a similar way, saying, "Write in a book all the words that I have spoken to you" (Jeremiah 30:2).

That is what I did. I searched through the journals to find these conversations which I marked with a "W" for "Word from the Lord" on the top of the page to find them easily.

The pages that follow recount some of these conversations with God, beginning with the first five times that I heard Him. I have these conversations with His words in italics.

God desires to have a relationship with you and to speak in personal ways. I want to encourage you in your spiritual journey with Jesus, the Great Shepherd of the sheep.

POWER IN PRAISE

The first time that God spoke to me was at our church in Anoka, Minnesota. In February 1981, during worship, a prophet spoke a word of prophecy to our congregation. After that, I sensed that the Holy Spirit had something more to say. I was prompted to write down the words:

> *As we are released in praise, power will come upon us, as the Lord Himself is power, and is in us. It is power released, and power to overcome whatever it is that is binding us. As you release yourself in praise, He will increase the power within.*

I showed these words to the woman who prophesied, and she confirmed that these words were from God. She encouraged me to speak out these prophecies for others' strengthening, encouragement and comfort, as stated in 1 Corinthians 14:3.

This was the beginning. The Lord was teaching me what His voice sounded like in my thoughts, and I was able to receive confirmation from this seasoned prophet. I was grateful to know that I could also hear from God. I experienced His Presence and peace as I praised Him and felt closer to God and anticipated more of His words.

GOD SPEAKS AGAIN

Over a year passed and, though I studied the Bible, prayed, and attended Bible school classes, my personal time of truly listening to the Lord was lacking. I felt frustrated and wondered why God seemed so distant. Thankfully, prophets in our church continued to speak out prophecies.

One day in June 1982, shortly after I graduated from the adult nurse practitioner program at the University of Minnesota, I met with the doctor who was my preceptor in the program. When I asked about the possibility of continuing to work at the clinic after my internship, he explained that there was no need for a nurse practitioner at that time. My hopes were dashed, because I enjoyed working there.

That evening, Mike and I went to a Bible study. I was discouraged about my lack of employment as a new nurse practitioner. This is what the Lord said to me through a prophet that night:

> You are bought by Me. You are no others' but Mine. And surely I would take the scissors and cut the ties between you and men. I would cut the security that would surround you so that you might know of the security in Me. And fret not at what I would do, even the wounding, for surely you shall be adorned with jewels and delight in that which I should do to replace that which I would take away. So fret not even in the pulling out of the chair from underneath you. Let yourself go in Me and I shall catch you. I am always there. I shall be that Rock, your undergirding, and you are established in Me.

The heavy burden that I had been carrying lifted immediately, and I experienced peace. I began to trust God more about my lack of employment.

Two months later, I re-read that prophecy and searched scriptures that seemed to go along with it. The first was John 8:36 which says, "So if the Son sets you free, you will be free indeed."

Next, the Lord impressed me to read Psalm 61:

Hear my cry, O God; listen to my prayer.²From the ends of the earth I call to you, I call as my heart grows faint; lead me to the rock that is higher than I.³For you have been my refuge, a strong tower against the foe.⁴I long to dwell in your tent forever and take refuge in the shelter of your wings.⁵For you, God, have heard my vows; you have given me the heritage of those who fear your name.

⁶Increase the days of the king's life, his years for many generations.⁷May he be enthroned in God's presence forever; appoint your love and faithfulness to protect him.⁸Then I will ever sing in praise of your name and fulfill my vows day after day.

After that, I read Psalm 62:

Truly my soul finds rest in God; my salvation comes from him. ²Truly he is my rock and my salvation; he is my fortress, I will never be shaken. ³How long will you assault me? Would all of you throw me down—this leaning wall, this tottering fence? ⁴Surely they intend to topple me from my lofty place; they take delight in lies. With their mouths they bless, but in their hearts they curse. ⁵Yes, my soul, find rest in God; my hope comes from him. ⁶Truly he is my rock and my salvation; he is my fortress, I will not be shaken. ⁷My salvation and my honor depend on God; he is my mighty rock, my refuge. ⁸Trust in him at all times, you people; pour out your hearts to him, for God is our refuge. ⁹Surely the lowborn are but a breath, the highborn are but a lie. If weighed on a balance, they are nothing; together they are only a breath. [10]*Do not trust in extortion or put vain hope in stolen goods; though your riches increase, do not set your heart on them.* [11]*One thing God has spoken, two things I have heard: "Power belongs to you, God,* [12]*and with you, Lord, is unfailing love"; and, "You reward everyone according to what they have done."*

The definition of security is "a place of refuge, safety, assurance, confidence, and hope." As I read these psalms, I personalized them to read, "Your soul will find rest in Me alone, Bonnie. Your salvation comes from Me. I alone am your rock and your salvation (the One who makes you whole). I am your fortress, and you will never be shaken. Find rest in Me alone, Bonnie. Your hope comes from Me. I alone am your rock and your salvation. I am your fortress. You will not be shaken. Your salvation and your honor depend on Me. I am your Mighty Rock, your Refuge. Trust in Me at all times, Bonnie. Pour out your heart to Me, for I am your refuge."

Psalm 32:7 says, "You are my hiding place; you will protect me from trouble and surround me with songs of deliverance."

After I completed this Bible study, God's words became more personal to me. As for employment, I relinquished the idea of getting a job at the clinic. I released the burden and trusted Him.

In November, while working at the hospital, I received a phone call from the director of that clinic. He wanted me to come in for an interview. That day, my eye was infected and I thought I looked terrible. Yet, the director offered me a nurse practitioner job, and I was elated.

NURSE PRACTITIONER JOB

Years had passed since I heard the Lord speak. During a spiritually dry time, I fought off depression. Even though I had a job at the clinic, I was not content. At age thirty-three, and after six years of marriage, we had no children and were in the midst of infertility testing. We were also dissatisfied with the church we attended.

In 1983, I experienced foreign medical missions while on a short-term trip to Uganda, East Africa. Everything else in my life seemed mundane in comparison. I thought that perhaps God would move us to the mission field in the fall of 1985, but no doors opened. I cried to the Lord, "Help! I'm miserable." He heard and answered my prayer. That evening, Mike and I were at a friend's home for a Bible study. Not knowing my circumstances, one of the prophets spoke these words:

Don't fret, My daughter, for the coming to pass of My Word. You shall bear the child which you have hoped for. You shall see My nature come forth in you. A ministry shall happen for you, so be in a believing stance. Your heart has grown weary and troubled with more than one care. I will take the burden from your heart. I would free your heart so a river of faith would flow. You shall have a new faith for things that you didn't think you had faith for in times past. I shall not leave you unfulfilled in this. I shall minister through you in both small and tall ways. Despise not the day of small beginnings. You are a mighty person of God.

That night when I copied this word to paper from a cassette, there seemed to be more that the Lord wanted to say to me. I took my journal and I wrote these words:

I have you in this job for a reason. You are to minister life and purpose to people that I bring your way. I have you in this place for My purposes. Grow not weary. Draw your strength from Me as you seek My face. Call on Me in times when you are burdened and weighed down with the cares of this world and the cares of your heart. I will touch and renew your heart. Cast your cares on Me and I will take them from you. I have you here for My purposes and soon you will know what those are. You will be with child, and it will not be a light thing. I will give you the strength to bear them.

As I look back over those words now, I am blessed to overflowing at their timeliness. God spoke and said that I'd be with child at a time when I worked in a clinic with pregnant women. He said His purposes would prevail for me. I now had the courage to continue.

I worked in the clinic for another nine months until I was laid off in May 1986. This unemployment, however, gave me an opportunity to go to Uganda, East Africa again in July 1986.

FOURTH EXPERIENCE:

PREPARING FOR UGANDA

The fourth time when God spoke to my spirit was on the plane to Uganda. Miraculously, an opportunity opened up for me to go on this short-term medical mission, and I was looking forward to the same thrilling trip I had in 1983.

On July 9, 1986, I flew from Minneapolis to New York, and to Amsterdam. Mike did not accompany me, as he thought that this trip was for me alone. In Amsterdam, I met one of my team mates, and we spent part of the day touring the city, which was great fun.

That evening when we arrived in the Amsterdam airport for the flight to Nairobi, Kenya, we met the rest of the medical team. The doctors and nurses were not all Christians, as I had expected. I was sorely disappointed, even shocked, when one of the nurses said, "I'm what you would call a heathen."

On the plane headed to Nairobi, I sat next to one of the women on the team whom I thought was Christian. However, something she mentioned caused me to question her commitment to the Lord. I felt alone and abandoned.

The plane took off just past midnight. I wrote in my journal shortly after takeoff. I had an impression that God had a purpose for me on this trip and it was not for my refreshment, but for others' gain. Jesus and those who had committed their lives to the Lord would be the only light on this team. I prayed, "Lord, give me the desire to work for You in Uganda."

I couldn't sleep because of inner turmoil. At 2:30 a.m., I wrote more in my journal and sensed God's words of encouragement welling up inside.

I know your need for fellowship, and I will provide this for you in Nairobi. Trust in Me and the plans that I have for you on this trip.

Mike is well taken care of, as is your cat. Your parents are not worried about you but trust Me to take care of you. I will work out the plans for this fall. It will all work out.

Don't worry about sharing Me with the team. Don't be concerned about the words. Remember how it worked out with the Dutch girl whom you witnessed to in the plane earlier? She was open to hearing your words. She was searching, and I am drawing her to Me. I will draw individuals to you and give you the words that they need to hear at the moment you speak them. Let Me lead the conversation. It will happen naturally so that it will seem supernatural.

There are those who are deeply hurt. I will open the door when they are ready to share. Pray for the right time. There are those who appear hardened, yet they are soft underneath. Be gentle with them. These are the ones you'll be 'licking back to health' as in the vision your pastor had of you before you left. You will be an overcomer of the evil forces that seek to destroy you and the words that I want you to speak. Call on Me during those times, and I will put the enemy under your feet. He will not come near you, because I have set My angels in charge over you, lest you dash your foot against a stone. You will not stumble or fall but will rise up victoriously. I am teaching your mind to war against the enemy.

Now that all is quiet, look back at what happened. Discouragement came because you felt alone and afraid that you were on the wrong trip at the wrong time. I have set you apart to be a shining light to those on your team. As others catch the light of My Spirit and are open to Me, the light will grow brighter. I will make this come about because it is the Light of My Son and My Spirit in you that will ignite others, and they will come to know the Son through you. In some, you will be planting seeds. In others, you will help to further their growth.

Be open to hear what I will say to you. You will be surprised that you can hear Me through all the clutter of your mind. As My voice grows stronger, the clutter will leave. The voice of My Spirit is there. Listen to it. Strain your ears to hear the still, small voice, and as you do, the thoughts of clutter will be stilled. The peace of My Spirit will then prevail. This is My mission, and I will fulfill it in you and through you. I love you and am here.

Indeed, this was a word in season which was worth more than gold! I was able to rest after hearing His voice. The Lord directed me to meet Christians in Nairobi and in Uganda who strengthened me. The following are a few examples:

- *The first Christian I met was Agatha from African Evangelistic Enterprise (AEE) who briefed us on the trip ahead and showed the film that I had also shown in my home church.*

- *Our team stayed at the guest house on the AEE grounds in Karen, Kenya, just outside of Nairobi. This place was named for Karen Blixen, whose life was depicted in the book and movie, "Out of Africa." Festus, a Christian who served us at the guest house, was a blessing. I stayed there on my birthday, and Festus made a cake with a "Happy Birthday" sign placed on a stick from a tree right in the middle of it.*

- *To my surprise, I met two Christian men that I knew while waiting at the Nairobi airport for a flight to Entebbe, Uganda. Days before, I prayed with Jesse and his wife in their home for our separate trips to Uganda. His friend, Charles, stayed in our home years ago.*

- *God amazed me with another divine appointment. He arranged for our group to be parked outside a large audito-*

rium in the center of Kampala, Uganda. Suddenly, I heard someone preaching the gospel inside. I was surprised when my teammates who were mostly non-believers wanted to come with me inside the auditorium. Jesse was preaching. When he saw me, he called me out of the audience to speak, play the guitar and sing! I was stunned but went forward. Our team heard the gospel that day.

- *After the meeting adjourned, a Ugandan nursing student approached me and asked if I'd speak at a Christian Student Nurses Association meeting. By this point, I was definitely strengthened by God's Holy Spirit.*

- *At the Namirembe Guest house, I met another Christian man from Florida. He came to fund and supervise the building of Christian schools. Every day we enjoyed fellowship together as we shared God's purpose for our trips.*

- *Once, the Youth With A Mission (YWAM) director in Uganda visited the guest house and gave me directions to the YWAM base in Jinja. On one of our days off, our team took a van and met him in Jinja for a tour. This was a dream come true, as I had hoped to see the YWAM base there but didn't know how that would ever happen. Mike and I had hoped to attend a YWAM Discipleship Training School when I returned from Africa.*

- *Another group of Ugandan girls who stayed at the guest house invited me to a Christian wedding, which I was honored to attend.*

God provided His people in Nairobi and Kampala, Uganda, as encouragement and support. I remembered God's word to me on the plane before arriving on African soil that God's purposes would prevail, and they did. He is so faithful!

As I looked back, I was blessed to see how God orchestrated the entire trip. I was grateful for that second opportunity to serve the people in Uganda, which helped to keep my vision for missions alive.

ATTITUDE ABOUT LEADERS

The fifth major time the Lord spoke to me came while I was attending the School of Primary Health Care through YWAM in 1987. I was in the village of Banaue, Philippines, on the northern end of Luzon Island among the picturesque mountainous rice terraces. At the same time, Mike traveled with the YWAM School of Community Development's mission trip to the Solomon Islands. We had peace about traveling separately so we could finish our training in the different schools we attended.

One day, our team was preparing for a trip to another village. The group leaders prayed and sensed that God wanted the team to delay the outreach that day. They thought we were not spiritually prepared. I agreed with this because I sensed heaviness inside over a church situation at home. When we prayed together as a team, I told the group that I was discouraged. Two others also admitted that they were discouraged. One of my teammates asked if I wanted to pray with her after the meeting. I gladly said yes. I told her about the situation in our home fellowship and why I wanted to leave that church. She asked me to consider three questions:

1) *Was it that I wanted to get away from what I disagreed with?*

2) *Was it that I was wronged and people didn't treat me properly?*

3) *Was it time to leave?*

I returned to my room. I had to know why I was discouraged and was thankful to spend all day with God to find out.

I wrote in my journal. My thoughts flowed, and so did God's thoughts towards me about the situation. I found the book by Joy Dawson called, *Intimate Friendship with God: Through Understanding the Fear of God*. One of the chapter's, "Touching the Lord's Anointed," stood out, and I knew I had to read it. The chapter began with the story of Moses and the Israelites. When the Israelites grumbled against their leader, Moses, they were actually complaining against God. The Lord spoke:

Bonnie, when you complained about your pastor, you are complaining about Me.

I asked God, "What did I complain about?" The Holy Spirit brought attitudes to my mind that I needed to confess. I prayed, "Lord, I repent. These are wrong and negative thoughts, and I am not to judge the pastor. When I complained, I was complaining about You."

Then I read in Exodus 17:8-13, how Joshua led the Israelites against the Amalekites. Moses, Aaron, and Hur went to the top of the hill overlooking the battlefield. As long as Moses held up his arms, the Israelites won, but when he lowered his arms, the Amalekites won. So, Aaron and Hur brought a stone for Moses to sit on, and they held up his arms until the sun went down. In this way, Joshua totally defeated the Amalekites.

God said:

Bonnie, you were not holding up your pastor's arms in prayer. Whenever you saw something you thought was done wrong, you complained to Mike about it or withdrew from your pastor. You ought to pray for him. I can only move on his behalf as you and others in the church support him in prayer and ask Me to give him wisdom.

I prayed, "Forgive me for my prideful and critical attitude, thinking my ideas were better than his. I forgive him for things he said or did that I believe hurt me."

In Numbers 11:10-31, Moses heard the people complain, so he also complained to God about all these people who seemed like babies to him. They kept whining for meat. Then God provided them with quail to eat. While they were still eating, He became angry and caused a severe plague to break out, and God destroyed the people who craved other food. I meditated on these scriptures.

Bonnie, you are acting like a child with your complaining. When you come to Me with your complaints, search your own heart first. Humble yourself before Me and come with a thankful heart. Learn from Me as to why I want you to stay in this church. I am molding your character, and part of what I am doing is to teach you to submit under leadership that I have placed over you. Allow Me to do My work, and you will be pleased. What your pastor does and says is My business. What I require of you is to submit under his authority, and I will work to change his motives and plans to fit My motives and plans for him and for the church under him.

I desire to teach you how to submit under authority even if that person is not doing what I want or does not meet your expectations. Don't look to man to be a perfect leader. People will always let you down. No one is perfect. You aren't either.

Leaders I have set over you will make mistakes. Are you willing to forgive them? They are learning from Me. The more they seek Me, the more like Me they will become in their leadership abilities. Be patient with them as I am patient with you. Don't turn from them or cut yourself off from them. That's not what I have for you. Your attitude when they make mistakes is what I am the most interested in right now.

I am working to change and perfect your heart. Don't expect to see a change. They may never change for you to see. I am requiring you to submit to this process of growth. I will work on your behalf to change your attitude. I want you to be humble and meek. Lean on Me and ask Me to help you. I understand more than you what problems exist. As you pray with the right motives and spirit for others involved, I will move to change these problems. I want to see justice done, even more than you.

Come to Me when you see that something is not right. Confide in Me what you sense in your heart. Come with a humble and thankful heart. Begin to look for the good in the leaders I have placed over you. The qualities are there, or else I wouldn't have brought them this far. They are My anointed. Treat them as such.

Be careful, Bonnie, when you murmur and complain against the Lord's anointed. You allow a foothold for Satan to plant seeds of strife and division. Stand firm against Satan with the right attitude and right heart towards the leadership, and then Satan can't have a foothold in this area. I will remind you of these words whenever you are tempted to rise up against your leaders by complaining and blaming them for things they do or say. I am leading you on this journey of faith. I set the circumstances and place you with the people. See the good in them and the qualities I have formed.

God showed me that the root was a rebellious attitude toward those in authority over me.

I am allowing you to see a pattern that was formed against leaders. Although you have not rebelled outwardly, you have turned away from them. I have shown these things to you in order to change this pattern of rebellion, so it will not turn into an outward rebellion. Please learn submission now. It will do you good. The lessons will be repeated if they are not learned. I am patient with you. Look at the character that Moses saw in Me. I am full of compassion and pity, and not easily angered. I show great love and faithfulness.

I read the story in the Bible about David and his submissive attitude toward King Saul (1 Samuel 18:9-24). Saul had it in his heart to kill David because he was jealous of David's popularity. Once, Saul was sitting in his house with a spear in his hand. He tried to pin David to the wall, but David dodged, and the spear stuck in the wall, while he ran away.

Saul's army moved from place to place while they pursued David. Once, Saul and his army even stopped at the cave where David's men were hiding (1 Samuel 24). David crept up unnoticed and cut off a corner of Saul's robe. Afterward, David was conscience-stricken for having cut off a corner of his robe. He said to his men,

"The Lord forbid that I should do such a thing to my master, the Lord's anointed, or lift my hand against him; for he is the anointed of the Lord" (1 Samuel 24:6).

After reading these passages, the Lord said:

From this incident, I want you to look at two things. David's conscience began to hurt. Saul was the king that the Lord chose, and David called him "Master" even though Saul tried to kill him. Saul's intent was murder. Other mistakes that your leaders make are small in comparison. David submitted to Saul, who in his heart was a murderer. This should be an example to submit to any leader that I place over you even if he is a murderer at heart. I am in control and will bring vengeance when it is due. You are not to harm any leader I have placed over you in what you do, say, or think. Evil actions come from what is in the heart. Your words can cause much damage. Cleanse your heart before you speak to any leader about his actions.

Regarding the scripture that said, "David's conscience began to hurt and he said, "May the Lord keep me from doing any harm to my master." Bonnie, let this be your prayer

to Me, and I will keep you from doing any harm to your leaders. Your flesh is weak. I understand that. I will not allow you to be tempted without a way of escape. I am your way of escape. Don't turn around and retreat away from your leader and take all of your rebellious thoughts with you. Instead, look to Me and ask Me to cleanse your heart, and I will create in you a clean heart toward your leader. I am showing you what is in your heart, including the pride in thinking you are justified. Humble yourself before Me, and I will lift you up. Come to Me for a thorough cleansing, and you can experience My Presence.

"Lord what does this mean? Is this about tomorrow's trip to the Ifugao village?"

He replied:

The Ifugao people don't worship Me, because they don't know Me yet. As you reveal My character to them, they will want to put away the things they have worshipped. They need to know that I am a loving God, full of compassion for them. They need to know about Jesus and how He was sent to bring reconciliation between them and Me. They need to be saved, but they also need to know how to be saved. Point them to Jesus, Who is the Way, the Truth, and the Life. Give them an opportunity to choose whom they will serve. You will see the fruit of your labor. I have brought you to this place. You are a living sacrifice for Me so that others may hear and know that I am the Lord. You won't be disappointed.

God dealt with me ever so gently and counseled me. I experienced the Lord's Presence once again.

The next day, our leaders said we were ready to go. We traveled by bus for an hour toward the Ifugao village. We stopped at a foot path and hiked for two hours through the rice terraces. God impressed upon me to look straight ahead because the path was narrow and rugged. A pool of water planted with rice was to the left, and there was a cliff that dropped off to my right.

That evening, after a day of holding a clinic in the village, one of the staff members led a Bible study on God. Through an interpreter, she gave a salvation message. One man received the Lord! He was wearing a "G" string and a suit coat. I will always remember him and his joyful countenance. The journey up the mountain was worth the effort.

After these five occasions of hearing God's voice, I kept journals and wrote in them almost daily. May the next chapters encourage you to seek God and hear with spiritual ears what He may say to you.

MISSIONS

BOY FROM THE DUMP

The Primary Health Care School I was part of traveled to the Balut YWAM base near Manila, Philippines. For one month, we students and a YWAM healthcare worker put on our rubber boots and hiked a half mile from the mission base to the city dump called Smokey Mountain. Rising some 120 feet from the valley floor, the mound of garbage covered approximately 24 acres. Most of the 30,000 residents who lived on the dump scavenged daily for food, additions to their living quarters, or something to resell, which may have been their only income.

On this particular day in August 1987, I was ready for my daily walk to the dump, but God had other plans for me. I heard a knock at the door, and a 12 year-old boy from Smokey Mountain stood there with his two friends. He wore a ragged T-shirt, shorts and sandals. He held his twisted wrist which caused his hand to hang in a lifeless position. He had fallen at a playground, and had come with his friends who knew about the YWAM mission base. Our medical team prayed for him, and my instructor asked me to help make a splint for his arm. Then, she said, "Bonnie, I want you to take him to the hospital. I'll call for a taxi."

When the taxi arrived, I asked the driver to stop at the dump. In hand motions, I asked the boy, whose name was Boy, if he would find his mother so she could go with us to the hospital.

I don't know why I became so attached to this boy. He didn't speak a word of English, yet we somehow understood each other.

At the hospital's crowded emergency room, Boy, his mother, and I looked on as a man was wheeled in next to us. He was unconscious and bleeding from his head wound. The staff searched his billfold to find out his identity. My stomach turned as we witnessed this incident. Finally, a nurse pulled a curtain to separate us from him.

After hours had passed, a doctor came to examine Boy's arm and ordered a nurse to start an IV. The staff told me that he would need to wait several hours for surgery, so his mother stayed, while I took a train to Balut.

I returned to work at the dump. That afternoon, Boy's grandmother found me and handed me a note which said, "Boy needs surgery to repair his broken arm, and his doctor needs more casting supplies. Can you buy and deliver them to the hospital?"

I went back to the mission base with his grandmother. One of the health care workers walked with us to a drug store and bought the necessary supplies, then, Boy's grandmother and I headed to the hospital to deliver them.

When we arrived, we found Boy and his mother. All of us were hungry. I found out that patients do not eat unless their family feeds them, so I bought supper.

After we ate, Boy's mother and grandmother stayed with him. I started the long journey on the train back to the base, only to be scolded that I was out past dark, and no one had known where I was. Discouraged, I sat up in bed that night with my journal, and tears streamed down my face. God said:

You are investing in this boy's future.

The words burned in me, and I wrote, "Relationships are what matter most and impact someone's life."

The next day, I asked my instructor if I could visit Boy in the hospital with his grandmother. She gave her permission. Boy grinned widely when he saw us. He was in a bed with his arm in a cast and strung up in a pulley. I noticed a cat under his bed, apparently to keep the mice population down. A doctor found us and explained that Boy could go home the next day when his bill was paid. The cost of his hospital stay, treatment, and surgery was $50 US. I told our leader, and the YWAM base paid the bill.

The following day, Boy's mother and I took a taxi to the hospital with the money. This time, we brought Boy home. Later that day when I visited Boy, he was all smiles. Many YWAMers and his friends signed his cast.

On my last Sunday afternoon in Balut, it rained fiercely. I decided to take a nap, but I couldn't sleep. I heard the Lord say:

Go visit Boy and his family and tell them about Me.

As much as I tried to ignore this prompting, I knew I couldn't get away from the Lord. I searched for a health care worker who spoke Tagalog, and we headed to the dump.

Through the pouring rain, we found Boy's makeshift house of old mattresses and cardboard. His grandmother, mother, and Boy welcomed us in. He smiled again as I shared through the interpreter how much Jesus loved them and wanted to be a part of their lives. Humbly, all three of them bowed their heads and prayed to ask Jesus into their hearts. As Luke 15:10 explains, there was much rejoicing by the angels that day.

When I arrived home, I exchanged letters with someone on the YWAM base who knew of Boy. I found out that someone in YWAM paid for Boy's education. Then I lost track of him. I heard that the dump later was cleared out and high-rise apartments were built instead. Some of the people found another dump site to live on.

For me, this was a short-lived experience. Yet, the words, "You are investing in the life of this boy's future" still ring in my ear. I believe that, to the Lord, this was a valuable mission. I entrusted Boy to God and prayed that seeds of faith were planted in his heart that still grow and produce fruit.

BEGINNING AGAIN

By August 17, I still had two weeks before returning to Hawaii. In the YWAM library, I found a cassette tape by a lady whom I had met in Hawaii before leaving on our mission trip. As I listened to the tape, I was touched and molded in a new way. I longed for more of the Lord. As the scriptures say, "As a deer pants for the water, so my heart longs after You." I noted my conversation with the Lord. "Where do I begin?"

It is time to put the Bible Study patterns aside. Begin now. Go slowly in your readings. Experience My Presence. Don't rush through My words. Understand My heart for you and for others. Know that I will lead you in this walk and show you what you need to do. Now is a new beginning. Lay aside the old pattern.

I knew I needed to put aside my routine pattern for reading portions of the daily Bible reading program. The words had become, lifeless. I knew what God meant when He said,

Begin now.

So, I started by reading Mark 1, and then I promptly fell asleep.

That night, I had a most wonderful dream, which I believe was from God. The scene was rice terraces in the rain, but the place was in America, not the Philippines. It was called Banaue but the people were Americans. There was one man who lived further up in the country. He was single, about 50 years old, and I was drawn to his dark eyes full of compassion. He had a ministry to the people in the town.

Several people drove to his house in the country. They seemed to be older, of working age. It was the end of a busy work day, yet the entire town gathered at the house. They couldn't come earlier because they were working themselves. I didn't see the man now, so I began to meet the needs of the people. One lady commented on how he and I made a good team. I thought of the scripture in Mark 1:33 which says, "And the whole town gathered at the door."

When I awoke, I realized that the man represented Jesus! The scripture I had just read in Mark relayed the story that after working all day, the whole town gathered at His door with all their needs. I prayed, "Jesus, when You saw the crowds coming, You did not turn them away, but met every need."

I thought about the man's character and who he represented in the dream. I knew that Jesus did not turn anyone away. He had a servant's heart of compassion on the multitudes who approached Him.

In the morning, I asked the Lord, "What are the lessons to be learned here?"

Note My personality and character. It is My personality that I want you to see as well as the relationship and compassion I had for the people of this town. I also want you to see your past. You are part of My ministry. When I wasn't there for a few minutes to meet the needs of the people, you began to do what you could. You also thought that you would do what you could until I returned.

Now, look at the man working on needs close to the house. Remember that the lady pointed him out and said that you and he made a good team. You are yoked to Me, and we work well together within My yoke. Look at the time of day this was. It was after the people had worked all day and they couldn't get away any sooner because of their schedules. They came in their cars and parked on the grass and gathered in the yard. They came to Me because they knew Me.

When you saw that you could do your part to help meet their needs, you were not tired. No matter how insignificant you thought their needs were, they were significant to the people. You helped to meet their needs, and they were drawn to you by your servant's heart. You knew that they would all leave because it would be getting dark, and they all had things to do at home. But I wanted them to go home satisfied, because they had received what they had come to Me for. It was insignificant to Me, but it was important to them. They came to Me, Jesus, and they knew that I would meet their needs.

Now, look at you. You fit right in. I had a place for you, and you were comfortable being the man's helper. The part you played in that ministry fit you. You knew that you could do the job. It came naturally to you. You were made to do that job, and it wasn't hard for you. You didn't have to struggle with it. Remember that My yoke is easy and My burden is light.

We are a team. I did the bulk of the work, which is similar to Me being the doctor and you being the nurse. I am the One with full responsibility and authority, and you are My helper. I will never require you to have the ultimate authority or responsibility. Although it seemed that the man you saw in the dream wasn't there initially, he was soon to arrive. After you began your work, you turned around, and I was there. I want you to look at the people and get involved in what you can do. An onlooker will notice Me and say that you and I make a good team.

As I turned back to Mark 1:32-33, a prayer welled up inside of me, "Oh, Jesus, I am glad to be Your helper. You are a tireless servant. You never complained that it was too late in the day to minister to people."

The scripture in Matthew came back to me, "My yoke is easy and My burden is light." Then the Lord said:

You came to the mission house to see what I did and then found yourself getting involved easily.

I prayed, "Thank You, for making me work the way I do. You created me with the character and skills I have. Put me where those skills can be utilized."

Ephesians 2:10 says, "For we are God's workmanship, created in Christ Jesus to do good works which God prepared in advanced for us to do."

The Lord continued to speak:

What you were doing did not involve medicine. You were helping your Master in what He was doing. You were not taking over. You knew that your Master was going to be the one doing the work. You were equipped to be His assistant. You were making order out of chaos. This is part of the ministry I have for you.

You are beginning to see My character through this dream. Concentrate on the personality of that man and see Me for who I am. I have his same eyes, the same gentleness and tireless, non-complaining character.

The dream began to fade, yet I believe that this was from God. When it became daylight, I knew I had been with the Lord. I saw a glimpse of His nature.

A few weeks later, I found a verse in Job 42:5-6 that reminded me of this dream and the conversation I had with God, "My ears had heard of you, but now my eyes have seen you." I caught a glimpse of God, just like Job, and had gained a new appreciation of Him. I had cried out for a revival during my time with Him, and He heard my prayer.

My relationship with God since then has been different. When I am not sure what to read, I reflect on a verse about guidance. Isaiah 42:16 says, "I will lead the blind by ways they have not known, along unfamiliar paths I will guide them; I will turn the darkness into light before them and make the rough places smooth. These are the things I will do. I will not forsake them."

When I am unclear about my purposes in life, I am reminded of another journal entry which I also believe was inspired by the Lord. I wrote, "My life is a tapestry of people and experiences. Each is a thread, hand-picked by the Lord to make of my life a work of His hand that will bring glory to my Maker and Designer on my final day. I do have a place in God's kingdom. I am uniquely tailored and designed by Him."

QUESTIONS ABOUT MISSIONARIES

On the last Sunday before leaving the Philippines, I walked toward "the dump" from the Balut YWAM base. As I traveled the familiar street, I noticed a building I hadn't seen before. The sign said, "The Norwegian C M and A Church" (Christian Missionary and Alliance Church). "Lord, why are missionaries from so many places leaving their nations to go to other countries? It doesn't make sense." He impressed on me:

Think of land as having no divisions but just being places on the face of the earth. Think of people as not having nationality divisions, but every person created is an individual born somewhere. Each person is born to a specific mother and father. These parents have a mother tongue. They are from a certain tribe and nation. You are of another tongue, tribe, and nation.

Jesus told us to preach the Word to every tribe, tongue, and nation. He is so faithful that when we ask Him a question, He provides answers. I smiled and was glad that for this time in my life, I heard the call to preach the Word to the Philippine nation.

LOOKING AHEAD TO MINNESOTA

Our YWAM team left the Philippines on August 25, 1987, bound for Hawaii. I had a short stay in Kailua-Kona, Hawaii, while waiting for Mike to return from the Solomon Islands. Our year with YWAM had come to an end.

The time in Hawaii was a spiritual oasis before heading back to Minnesota and the familiar, workday life. Mike would return to work, and I would be looking for employment as a nurse practitioner. We would probably sell our house in Anoka and move to St. Paul to be closer to his new job location which had changed from the suburbs to the inner city. As it was, his drive from Anoka to St. Paul would be a 45-minute commute each way.

I was apprehensive to leave a time of ministry and spiritual highlights in my life for unknowns back home. Only God would know our future.

On August 27, when I spent quiet time with God, I turned to Joshua 1:9 which says, "...Be strong and courageous. Do not be terrified; do not be discouraged, for the Lord your God will be with you wherever you go." What a great promise. He said,

> *Don't be discouraged about returning to Minnesota. I will never leave you or forsake you. I will guide you every step of the way. Whether you go to the left or to the right, I will be the One who says, "This is the way, walk in it." Meditate on My word in the morning and before you go to bed.*
>
> *Fenelon's book will be a devotional book while you are here.[1] This will be a special time of spiritual rest and refreshment for you in Hawaii. Take advantage of it. Slow down and be reflective. I will guide you as to what to do each day. My direction will not be harsh or difficult but will bring*

---

[1] Fénelon, *Let Go* (Monroe, PA: Banner Publishing, 1974).

*you inner peace. Everything will fall into place. You will
know My direction for you by the time you meet up with
Mike. The travel agent recommended to you in the YWAM
office will help you. I will tell you when to go and see her.
Ask her about Kauai as well.*

*I have a special reunion planned for you and Mike. You
are going to love it. Mike is safe. He will be home in a week.*

I took time for reflection over what had transpired during our year in YWAM. I looked forward to what God had at home. I sought God for direction in my relationship with Him. This is what He said:

1) Pray for Mike daily. Ask him, "How can I pray for you?"

2) Each year you will have a 'watch word' beginning on August 18, your wedding anniversary. Your first year is, 'The Year of Inner Peace'. You are not to strive over traditions and rituals in your walk with Me. The kingdom within you is relaxed. Put patterns aside. Go slowly in your readings. Don't rush through My words. Know that I will lead you.

3) Have a separate notebook. Record the story in Mark 1:33 and verses that have special meaning.

4) Write out the songs that are meaningful to you. Make note of the chords and play them on the piano for Me.

5) Study a book about traditions and customs during the times of Jesus and Paul.

6) Write a list of books or tapes that are of significance and what you have learned.

For forty years, we have continued to pray for one another. I receive a watchword each August 18, for the year ahead. I kept a separate notebook with some of my favorite songs, which has been beneficial for praise and worship.

On Sunday, I went to a church service where God spoke to me during the pastor's sermon,

If you isolate yourself, the wounds will go deeper. I will bring you true fellowship and heal your wounds. As you walk in obedience, you will be made whole.

That afternoon, I pondered what the Lord said and studied the book of Acts about the New Testament Church. I knew that the Lord was getting through to me about our church back home. I searched through Acts and found that one of the purposes of the church is to strengthen one another in the faith. I listed twelve people who attended our church who were part of the original group. I asked the Lord to humble me and committed to love and serve them. This act of my will was important in preparation for the return to Anoka.

Mike returned to Kailua-Kona, Hawaii, from the Solomon Islands on September 3. On September 7, we flew to the island of Kauai, for a short trip before flying home. The money was provided in the exact amount needed by a supporter from church.

We rented a car and drove around the island. I was struck by its beauty. The contrast between blue sky, green slopes, and the teal ocean was spectacular. But we grew irritated with one another because I drove a stick-shift car with difficulty. I had a strong sense that we needed to get this resolved quickly.

We stopped at a lighthouse, talked about the issue, and prayed. It wasn't until we were on the Powerhouse Road that I understood this lesson: God is holy and cannot tolerate sin. We are to be holy too, to maintain unbroken fellowship with Him and with one another. After praying, we experienced a closeness and peace.

The next morning, there was an emptiness inside which I didn't understand. I journaled and said, "Lord, what is it?"

Get your eyes off your problems and onto Me.

The heaviness suddenly lifted. Words of a song came to mind, "Turn your eyes upon Jesus. Look full in His wonderful face. And the things of earth will grow strangely dim, in the light of His glory and grace." We finished our tour of Kauai, including the island's amazing Grand Canyon in all its glory.

HOMEWARD BOUND

We returned home from Hawaii in the middle of September, and our fantastic year in YWAM ended. I now entered a desert experience. While paging through my journal, I was clinging to God for His direction and strength. I received the following from God:

As you submit to Me, you will see a fulfillment of My word in your life.

I pondered these words as I prepared for church the first time since we returned. The sermon was on the will of God. I recalled some of the promises that the Lord gave me about children and true fellowship. I also remembered my promise to Him to love and serve the people at this church until He moved us.

The words that I recorded in my journal on that Sunday provided encouragement to me at a time of despondency and depression, "God gave me hope and has a way through any challenging situation. Satan tried to convince me that suicide was the only option. I would be out of my circumstances, but death is permanent."

I knew that if it is God's will for His divine purpose to keep me in the same job and church, then I could ask Him to show me what He has for me there. I realized I can cling to hope as an anchor that, in the fullness of His time, and in His purposes, He can change my attitude so that I can rest in Him. When His purposes are complete, then He may move me forward into something else for His benefit. These words were a "breathing hole" in a dark time.

HOUSES OR LANDS

We put our house up for sale at the end of October, believing that the Lord was leading us to a home closer to where Mike's work. His office had moved to downtown St. Paul while we were in Hawaii. Our house in Anoka sold in five days! We looked for houses in the St. Paul area. On October 31, 1987, we saw one in Vadnais Heights that we liked; however, it was out of our price range. I became discouraged, and asked the Lord, "What is Your view on this?" I sensed these words:

> Is a big, expensive house really what you want? What would you be sacrificing money-wise if you ended up going into debt to buy a house and had a large house payment? My long-term goals for you still stand. If you become preoccupied with your house, which will soon pass away, your eyes will focus on the wrong place. Your house should not be your primary concern, but instead a location, neighborhood, and the house within your means that I have for you. Don't look for a house that needs work, but one that requires little upkeep. I would not have you spend your time on material possessions, but on work within My kingdom. I will give you a house that is comfortable and one in which people sense My Presence and peace. Wait for it. Do not act on impulse or pressures from outside sources. Stop and wait for my direction. I won't lead you astray or let you make a serious mistake. Gain wisdom and understanding from Me. I will lead you to the right counselors, because there is wisdom in having many. Calmness and tranquility in your inner being is what I desire for you.

On Sunday, November 8, Mike and I went to our realtor's open house. He worked with the seller of another house that seemed right for us. We prayed and had peace about signing a purchase agreement on the home which we looked at on October 31. We had peace about that neighborhood.

Later that Sunday afternoon, our realtor called and said that the sellers did not accept our offer, but we could counter offer. We dropped to our knees and prayed. What came to Mike was that whenever his dad or grandfather made a deal, and it was counter offered, they would split the difference and counter offer again. Just then, our realtor called. We presented our counter offer, and heard that they'd have to think about it. We asked the Holy Spirit to guide us. Our realtor called and said that they accepted our counter offer. The house was ours. Praise God! We joined hands in a grateful time of prayer and celebration.

These words were impressed in me:

You have much to be thankful for. Don't let anyone put bondages and rules on you. I will lead you by My Spirit within you. That is what you just experienced. Come to Me in silence first. Don't try to re-direct your thoughts to be more spiritual. Bring your thoughts to Me and let Me re-direct them.

MOVING ON

The closing for our house in Anoka was December 20, and the purchase of the new one was set for January 15. The days were filled with packing boxes, preparing for a move, and beginning a new chapter in our lives. On our last Sunday at church, we asked the elders and pastors to pray for us, as we had been part of this congregation for eight years. During this prayer time, prophesies, and visions were given.

Our pastor said, "The steps of a righteous man are ordered of the Lord and He delights in His ways. I ask that Mike and Bonnie's steps would be ordered by the Lord. Holy Spirit, send them to Vadnais Heights with the joy of the Lord. I pray that they will know that they are in the purposes of God at this season of their life. God, you are going to bless them and direct them because their heart is in you. Thank You for them. I ask that everything will go smoothly with the closing process, and they will have much joy as they depart."

One of the other men in our church prophesied:

I am pleased this day with you. I have done a work in you, so you will emanate My glory. Your relationship is of My own handiwork. This year, look forward with joy for that which I have planted within you. For it truly reflects My nature. Faint not, but rejoice. I am doing a good work within you. It is true that the steps of a righteous man are ordered of the Lord. The steps you will take in the days ahead are of Me. I shall confirm them. I will establish the steps that you shall take. Know that the desire that leads you is not of your own self. I have led you. My daughter, fear not for that which shall come forth from within you. My word does not return to Me void.

Our pastor also had a prophecy:

For there will come a season in your life very shortly when you will feel isolated and alone. Know that I am bringing you into divine tutorship. You shall hear Me and know Me like you've never before. This is a time of enlargement in your hearts. I'm going to do a work of maturing in a great way, for I love you. Doubt it not, for this is My will. It is My plan that you are leaving. At times you will have doubts and fear. I am going to enlarge your ways, and the end will be greater than the former.

Another person said, "You have left a part of your heart in the places and congregations you have been involved in. This was part of the purifying process that God has done in each of your lives. God will prepare you for the work He has planned for you to reach out with the gospel to others.

Someone else had the following vision, "I saw a garden with green plants. The Lord was taking one plant and placing it in another location. The roots were not exposed.

There would be other plants placed in the hole that was left. The plants were green and bearing fruit in the entire process. Here is the meaning. You are represented by the plant that was being transplanted from one place to another within the same garden. The garden represents the church as a whole. The places represent different congregations. As you are being carefully uprooted by the Lord in one place, He has prepared a place for you in another. He will bring in another person or persons to fill in the local church you will be leaving."

Although we were packed and ready to move, the people buying our house in Anoka had problems with their loan going through, so we lived on the little we had not packed until we heard differently.

The first days in January, 1988 were peaceful. Mike continued his employment; however I was not working.

On January 10, we went to a church which had been recommended to us by someone in Hawaii. We loved it! I attended a ladies Bible study on Wednesday mornings and an aerobics class at the church on Tuesday nights.

The loan went through for the people to buy our house in Anoka. On January 13, the closings on both houses were held. Our moving days went smoothly and we were blessed by those who helped us.

January through March 1988, was a time of reading scripture, praying, and reading several books including one on the life of Madam Guyon, and another by Fenelon, both French Mystics.

In looking back at those three months, I realized I was struggling with depression because of my circumstances. Change, even good change, can be difficult and require adjustment. During those early months in our new house, I didn't work as a nurse practitioner.

We were married over eight years still had not conceived, so we met with an infertility specialist. After two surgeries for endometriosis, six months of hormone treatment, and testing for Mike, the doctor said there was nothing more he could do and encouraged us to adopt. After hearing this news, more depression set in.

In February, I attended a women's retreat. I recorded in my journal:

> *I have set aside this time for seeking Me. That is why you don't have a job. I don't mean for you to have idle time. I long to have you spend time with Me. Your joy will be made full only in fellowship with Me. When that time is over, you'll be ready in your spirit to go out and do what I want you to do. Understand what My will is for you during this time. If you find work that is not My work for you, you will be dissatisfied, and it won't be My best for you. Learn to trust Me with your life and praise Me with piano and voice. Learn to worship Me and sing a new song.*

RELIGION OR JESUS

The neighborhood we moved to included devoutly religious people of various denominations. One neighbor had a large portion of the truth about Jesus, but it seemed to be tainted by her denominational beliefs. Yet, I know I was called to love and accept her, and be a good neighbor.

My prayer was, "Lord, how do I share with her about a relationship with Jesus?" In a vision I saw a garden full of weeds and one tiny, stunted rose. This neighbor was watering the weeds, because she liked them, and she hardly noticed the flower. She didn't see anything wrong with the weeds. I asked the Lord, "Can't I chop away all the weeds so the rose can grow?"

> *No, she'd be angry with you.*

"What should I do?"

> *Water the rose so it will grow. As she realizes the beauty of the rose, she will notice the difference and will chop down the weeds.*

"But don't the weeds have roots?"

Be her friend. Give her plenty of space. The weeds repre-sent her religious beliefs that have little truth, and mostly tradition. The rose represents Jesus, the Rose of Sharon. The watering can is her church which teaches some truth.

"What about our neighbors across the street?"

You'll be good friends with them. This is where My love will be shown in greatest measure. Be their friend and spend time with them.

JOB INTERVIEW

In March 1988, I had a nurse practitioner job interview. Before I went for the second interview, I looked up scrip-tures on the words, "to be clean." In I John 1:9 and, Mark 7:23, the word, "deceit" stood out. I asked the Lord, "When was I deceitful?"

You were not honest about Me.

"Please clarify that, Lord."

Let them ask the questions. When you go for the second interview, let Me answer their questions through you. You are uncomfortable with the question about minors not hav-ing parental consent. I will guide you. Don't fear what their reaction might be or how you will answer. Trust Me. Provide the information they requested about your past volunteer experience.

Though I was not hired for that nurse practitioner job, I had peace, knowing that I had repented and obeyed Him. When something was off the mark between God and me, I was uncomfortable until He would shine His light on it. When that happened, I repented, and ask Him to cleanse me.

HOPE IN THE FORM OF A ROBIN

One morning in March, I saw a robin, and instantly a ray of hope welled up inside. The Lord inspired me to write, "I saw a robin today, the first one of the season. It meant that spring is coming after a long winter. Jeremiah 29:11 says, 'For I know the plans I have for you,' declares the Lord, 'plans to prosper you and not to harm you, plans to give you hope and a future.'"

My prayer was, "Thank You for thoroughly cleansing me of the past conflicts, and not allowing me to keep them hidden in a closet like a skeleton. As someone said, 'A skeleton will kick the door open at the most awful, inopportune time. Deal with it now or it will continue to surface.'"

The Lord said,

I'll show you what to do and say.

Isaiah 30:21 says, "Whether you turn to the right or to the left, your ears will hear a voice behind you saying, 'This is the way; walk in it.'"

I listed every issue that was problematic that I had never dealt with. That very night at an evening conflict resolution seminar, the topic was, "Forgiveness versus Bitterness." Even the seven steps to turn bitterness into forgiveness were helpful. I went through the steps outlined in the seminar, and another layer of bitterness dissolved, and I was grateful.

RESTING AND NESTING

A group of us from church attended the week long day seminar on conflict resolution. Before the meeting began, my friend turned to me and said, "In a dream I had last night, you were pregnant."

That evening, Mike and I attended the seminar. The author of the manual spoke in person. He shared insight from couples he counseled who struggled with infertility. These are the points the speaker offered:

- *Totally submit this desire to the Lord.*

- *Be totally free from tension, as tension hinders conception. Be at rest.*

- *Have melodious music in the home.*

- *Go to the elders, as James 5 states, and have them anoint you with oil, for the purpose of raising up a godly seed.*

At this point, one of the ladies turned to me and said, "Have you been prayed for and anointed with oil yet for infertility?" I replied that we had not.

God was working to bring a rest for my soul. I rejoice even now, when looking back to that depressing winter, that I was able to look forward to spring and new beginnings.

I took to heart what my friend said about having the elders anoint us with oil and pray about getting pregnant. I called our church office and made an appointment with the associate pastor. The earliest time he had available was on Monday evening, April 11, so we scheduled for that time.

IT IS ENOUGH

On April 4, I prayed and read from Gene Edward's book, The Early Church.[2] Two phrases stood out to me:

- *Utter abandonment.*

- *Drop everything to gain the depths of the riches of knowing Christ.*

My response in prayer was, "How do I do that, Lord? I long for You so much. Yet, here I am in St. Paul. What are we doing here? What about a nurse practitioner job? I have no desire for that."

It is enough for you to do the wash, the ironing, cooking and cleaning. It is enough for you to be wife for Mike. It is

---

[2]Gene Edwards, *The Early Church (Goleta, CA: Christian Books 1974).*

enough for you to know Me and spend time with Me. You'll know when the right door will open and for you to walk through. Don't look so far ahead. My grace is sufficient for you, and My mercy is new every morning.

The next two days, I wrote about the heart, soul, mind, and spirit. This Bible study ended with a heart-felt prayer: "Lord, You bring strength into my life on my spiritual journey. You use others to encourage me by their phone calls, visits. You know when I need to rest beside still waters. You know when a battle with the enemy is approaching and give rest."

One verse was significant, "But if ... you seek the Lord your God, you will find Him if you look for Him with all your heart and with all your soul" (Deuteronomy 4:29, AMP).

I am thankful for this stage of life. My concerns were:

- *Playing piano on Sunday for the next three weeks, and that this would bring good results.*

- *Having no children. I prayed, "Help me to be content without children."*

- *Having no job. My prayer was, "Thank You for helping us live within our means."*

TOTAL ABANDONMENT TO GOD

I listened to a lady's testimony on cassette tape. She was filled with utter joy because her troubles caused by resisting God had ended, and she lived in continuous joy. She had a sense of God's timing in her life each day. She enjoyed a blissful experience in God. A prayer welled up, "Show me my heart. Something is missing—I haven't surrendered. Jesus, I'm so afraid that I'll fail You and go my own way."

A scripture came to mind: "It is God who works in you to will and act according to His good purpose" (Philippians 2:13).

What is abandonment? I turned to similar scriptures and prayed, "I surrender all to Jesus, and cast all my cares upon You."

SURPRISE FROM THE LORD

On the morning of April 11, I woke up at 5:45 a.m. after sleeping all night, which was very unusual. I went into the study and sang to the Lord. I sat there for fifteen minutes. The Lord said,

That's it. You can go back to bed now.

It was 6:00 a.m. and Mike woke up. We had a special time together, and I had a sense that all that had happened was His plan.

The rest of the day was peaceful. I prepared my resume and sent letters to local clinics inquiring about a nurse practitioner job. The date on that resume was April 11, 1988.

That evening, we drove to church to meet with the pastor so he could pray and anoint us with oil so that we could conceive.

FORGIVENESS AND CLEAN BEFORE THE LORD

In our meeting with the pastor, we prayed and asked the Lord to lead the session. One of the first questions he asked was about my relationship with my father. I wondered why he focused on me first. He wanted to discuss many of my past attitudes toward my father, and other memories of my childhood. There were some things that I had never dealt with.

We talked about why I ran from one thing to another and from one relationship to another. I realized I avoided conflict all the time. So, whenever I'd run into a situation that I didn't like or agree with, I'd quit. That's why I was never satisfied with my jobs. I didn't want to complain, so

I resigned and found another job. Whenever I had a relationship with a young man, the same thing had happened. I told him about the many relationships I had before I met Mike. Mike already knew these things. I had gone from one relationship to another, seeking love to fill a void in my life. But when conflicts came up, I always ended the relationship.

The pastor helped me to see that I had emptiness inside, and that void could only and completely be filled with the Lord, Jesus Christ and His love for me. He asked me to forgive all the men I had ever known. He asked me to forgive myself and pray, asking the Lord to forgive me for the things I had done. So, for the first time I could remember, I forgave each one, forgave myself, and asked the Lord to forgive me for these things.

Then, the Lord spoke through our pastor:

The Lord loves you. I bless you. I love you My daughter. I have called you and have known you in your mother's womb, even before the earth was formed. I have a place for you.

He asked me to forgive my father for anything he had or hadn't done to demonstrate fatherly love to me. I forgave him for any ways he hadn't shown love to me.

After this, we talked about our marriage and he asked us individually what we thought about my relationship with my father and other males I dated before Mike. I don't remember exactly what was said, but I knew that these issues were helpful in understanding some conflicts that we had. He asked me to forgive Mike for things that he had or hadn't done in our marriage, and then, he asked Mike to forgive me for things I had or hadn't done in our marriage. Mike prayed about these issues, forgave me, and forgave himself for any judgment he had of me regarding my past relationships.

The pastor anointed our heads with oil and prayed over us. I left that office feeling forgiven and clean. Our time in his office must have been three hours. But the peace in our hearts was worth it all!

Hoping to become pregnant, we did everything that we could medically. There were tests for both of us, medicines I took for endometriosis, which is one cause of infertility, plus surgeries to remove endometriosis tissue on the outside of my uterus, fallopian tubes, and part of one ovary.

One year, a guest pastor had said to me, "It is not all that man can do, but it is that which is from God."

So, we had done all that "man" can do. I looked for all that the Lord could do.

It had been an intense two years. We had completed a year in missions and had traveled extensively from July 1986, to September 1987, then sold our house and moved in January 1988. I was physically and mentally exhausted. The Lord used the time in our new home from January to April 1988 as a resting and nesting period for me personally, free from the responsibility of a job, and free from many outside pressures. There was the excitement of a new house, new church, new neighborhood, and then the final emotional healing necessary between Mike and me as our pastor guided us through forgiveness, cleansing, and then anointing us with oil. It was a new start in our marriage and freedom from past patterns and hurts.

I explained our desire to have a child to my friend, a pediatrician. On April 16, 1988, I received this response in a cassette tape:

"The Lord is waiting until the healing has been done between you two before a child is conceived. God is going through these healings so you as a person and you as a couple can grow stronger. Marriage is a type of the relationship between Jesus and us. He builds strong marriages. He is building for you and Mike the beautiful foundation to then set in the jewel of a child or children. I just see it. It is almost as if He's painted a picture for me of seeing that in your lives, too. I know it is difficult to wait for children to come, but stand on the promises He's given you. He means it."

As part of the infertility testing, I checked my temperature daily and charted this for my doctor. Ovulation most likely has occurred if the morning temperature dips. When the temperature continues to rise after that, then most likely the woman is pregnant. My temperature dipped on April 11, and continued to rise after that. Could this be it, Lord? Could I be pregnant after nine years of marriage?

I recalled a Bible study we attended five years before. At the end, we prayed for one another. When it came time for them to pray for us about getting pregnant, I took notes as to what people said:

- *"The Lord will do a new thing in your home."*
- *"You shall have parents' hearts."*
- *"It will cause you to grow."*
- *"It will be glorifying to God."*
- *"It will be in His timing."*
- *"We shall have a family in the timing of the Lord."*
- *"Don't fear."*
- *"It shall not take away from your relationship but will add to it and make you grow in God."*
- *"I see children, "Twins!"*
- *"You shall have the heart of parents."*

These became God's words and promises that we would have children.

A JOB FOR YOU

One weekend we drove to Rochester, Minnesota, to visit Mike's parents, brother and sister. I was confused and anxious about my lack of employment, especially since Mike was encouraging me to find a nurse practitioner job.

The previous week, I had interviewed at two clinics. The next morning, April 23, the Lord woke me up before 6:00 a.m. I spent time with Him and asked Him about my job situation. I heard Him say,

You don't have to decide now.

That was it, but His words freed me from my anxiety.

When we arrived home, I received a call from an OB-GYN clinic which was only a mile from our home. They wanted me to come in for an interview. I was elated!

On Monday, April 25, just two days after I prayed about this, I had the interview. Of all things, during the interview, the doctor was called on his pager to the hospital for a delivery. He asked me to come along. I went to the hospital with him, scrubbed up, and watched as he delivered a baby.

When we returned to the clinic, the doctor offered me the job. I was to start May 2. My spirit soared. I do remember being nauseated at the clinic, possibly from some food cooked in a microwave. I began to wonder, could I be...?

MOTHER'S DAY

I was never this late with my menstrual period before. When I saw my aunt the day before Mother's Day, I told her I might be pregnant, and she said I had a glow on my face. How ironic that would be, to work at a job where I would see pregnant women and finally be pregnant as well.

I was flying high that day with the thought that I might be pregnant. Mike surprised me with a red rose on the kitchen table that morning with a card which said, "Happy Mother's Day."

That Sunday evening, we attended a church service in North St. Paul. The pastor spoke on "Time for Changes." How fitting, in the event of possibly having a new life growing within me. Wonderful words of life were spoken, as the pattern for coping with change began to unfold. The speaker invited those who were going through changes to come forward. Mike and I went up and knelt at the altar. We surrendered our lives again to the Lord. Serenity was definitely the spirit that prevailed. God said,

You don't know what's ahead for you.

I raised my left hand in surrender. I didn't realize it with my eyes closed, but the pastor stood behind us and prayed, "Lord, draw them to you." I felt knitted together with Mike. "It is time for a family" we said, and the pastor said, "It is time for the fulfillment."

There was much rejoicing, dancing, and praising God in that church. The worship team led us into the song, "Thou Hast Turned My Mourning into Dancing." I could envision David and Jesus dancing to that song, just as we did that night. I cried for joy, just as I had when years ago, a visiting pastor gave me a prophetic word about being a mother. He said, "And from your womb, shall you bear a child."

NOW I KNOW I AM PREGNANT

On Friday, May 13, I went to my doctor's office for a pregnancy test. It was positive! The nurse figured out that our baby's tentative due date was, January 8, 1989. The date of conception was April 11, the day that pastor prayed for us. The seed was planted that morning, and with prayer, forgiveness, and being anointing with oil, pregnancy followed. From the hallway, I called to Mike, who was waiting in the waiting room. I asked him to come into the hall and said to him, "Hi, Daddy!" He said, "Hi, Sweetie!" Overjoyed, we hugged and kissed, right there in the hall.

The rest of the day and weekend were spent telling relatives we were expecting our first child and writing their responses in a separate baby book. That day we also drove to Clintonville, Wisconsin, where we shared our news with Mike's brother and his family along with Mike's parents.

WAIT ON THE LORD

As I sat down to spend time with the Lord on June 1, I sensed that the Lord had something to say to me:

Grow strong in Me through the help of My saints. The resistance you sense is not of Me. Be strong against the wiles of the devil. Wait on My perfect timing and I'll come to you with the answer.

Wait on Me in the early part of the day. Don't look to others for advice. Still your soul and wait silently. Enter into My rest that I have for you.

Don't worry about your lack of sleep, for it will be returned to you later as you need it. My kind of "rest in the Spirit" as you reach that place, will be sufficient for you.

I know your frail body and its needs. I know you are with child. I've created both of you and know what your bodies need. I love you, My child. I long to wrap My arms around you, comfort you, and take you by My hand to still waters. I will restore your soul for service that will not weary you, because My yoke is easy and My burden is light.

Come, drink of the water that will refresh you. Come to the table of feasting before you. You are strong in My Spirit, though weak in your own strength.

Look for Me within you. There you'll find the relationship with Me that you long for. It is not in seeking the relationship others may have. Look within you to find Me there.

After the Lord spoke these words to me, I thought of words to a song, "My kingdom is within you. Be still. I'll meet you there. Be still and find Me there." I sang it softly as God sang it to me.

SEND DOWN YOUR ROOTS

We went to see a prophet at our former church on September 16. After the sermon, he prophesied to us:

So you're home! Well then, send down your roots and get established. Don't run here and there. Be established in God. This is the area of your laboring. Now I will make you field missionaries, even home missionaries. Many see out in the distant but cannot see that over which they stumble. So there is a ministry of home missions. Forget it not. And surely I will cause you to minister bread of life to those that have eaten of the wrapper and the chaff long enough. I will give you bread to feed to the hungry. I will give even meat to those who are more advanced. But know this. Send down your roots and be grounded because the wind blows. Be not concerned. For every time the storm comes and passes, the ground does loosen. Yea, send down your roots, and you shall be established with an establishment that you didn't know was possible.

The next day, I pondered what the Lord spoke to us. It cut to my core. I longed to be established in God, have a firmer foundation and deeper roots in Him when the storms come. I was drawn to the people at this church.

PREGNANCY GONE AWRY

Medical complications began in the sixth month of this pregnancy. On October 15, Mike's family had a baby shower for me in Rochester Minnesota. When I looked at the pictures from this second baby shower, I noticed that my ankles were quite swollen. Yet, I felt fine, and was still on cloud nine being pregnant.

I went to work on Monday, October 17, at the OB-GYN clinic and saw only a few patients. I went home early, sensing a cold coming with head congestion and sore throat. In the mirror, my face appeared swollen, which seemed odd. The next day, my cold seemed worse, with more head congestion and a still swollen face, so I stayed home from work.

At 28 weeks pregnant, I had an appointment with my doctor on Wednesday, October 19. The doctor noticed that I had 3+ protein in my urine, which was a significant amount. A pregnant woman should not have any protein in her urine. He explained that something was wrong with my kidneys, and they could not process large amounts of protein. I already had a deformed right kidney that was only functioning to one-third of its capacity due to repeated kidney infections. He asked me to do a 24-hour urine collection test. This test, along with my other symptoms of high blood pressure, weight gain, and fluid retention, indicated probable preeclampsia, which can cause significant danger for the mother and baby. He made an appointment with an OB-GYN physician for the following week.

The next day, I went to work. My co-worker, who was the physician's assistant, noticed that my ankles were swollen. I had continued to gain weight with fluid retention. A urine test, showed 4+ protein, which was worse than before. At that point, the treatment for a pregnant woman at that point is bed rest or admission to the hospital for bed rest and observation. Somehow, I was oblivious to the danger in that moment.

On Saturday, Mike and I went to the clinic to drop off my 24-hour urine collection in a large brown jug. More tests were taken for kidney function. Later, we drove to Stillwater for dinner on the Minnesota Zephyr train. One of the doctors whom I worked with in the OB-GYN clinic had given me two tickets because he and his wife couldn't attend. The train was filled with other OB-GYN doctors and their guests, so I determined that if anything further went wrong and the baby had to be delivered quickly, I would have several competent physicians to do the job!

Mike and I had a wonderful five-course meal on the train. He stopped to take my picture by the train. When I look at that picture now, I can hardly recognize myself, because my face was so swollen, and I was wearing large sun glasses. My light aqua rain coat was very loose, so I looked much heavier than I actually was. When we returned home, I cleaned the house. Mike snapped a picture of me while I relaxed in the new rocking chair by the fireplace.

The next day, Mike and I attended a Sunday school class at a different church. We met more people, and seemed to fit right in.

That evening, we went back to that church. A lady behind us introduced herself. When she noticed that I was pregnant, I explained that I had some medical concerns and she offered to pray for us.

On Monday, October 24, my work day was routine, although my blood pressure was high. That I continued to retain fluid was obvious in my hands, feet, and face.

The next day, I went to work at 10:00 a.m. to see one patient and stayed until noon to get caught up on charting. When I left that day, I wondered if I'd ever be back to work.

Since the previous Friday, I had recorded my blood pressure readings, and could see that they were getting progressively higher, and the protein level in my urine remained at 4+. Before I dropped off these records at my doctor's office that Wednesday, October 26, I shopped for groceries and dropped off my library books. I went home to rest and wait for the doctor to call. I rested on my left side to promote better kidney blood flow just as I urged my pregnant patients when they had similar symptoms.

As I expected, my doctor called shortly after I came home. He wanted me on bed rest until I saw the OB-GYN specialist on Friday. I called my co-worker to let her know I would not be coming to work.

Later that day, my mom came with a neighbor from their home in Akeley, Minnesota. Dad stayed home. We planned on doing early Christmas shopping. Mom decided to cook Swedish meatballs for supper, as this was one of my favorite dishes. I stayed on the couch all evening.

DREADFULLY ILL

Throughout the night, I had severe upper stomach pain and nausea. Attributing the pain to the Swedish meatballs, gravy, and heavy pepper seasonings, I took antacids. Never before had I experienced such excruciating pain. I spent much of the night vomiting, chewing antacids, and drinking milk. The night seemed endless.

At 5:30 a.m., I woke Mike up and shared about my stomach pain, nausea, and vomiting. I asked him to pray for me, and as he did, I felt better.

During the day, I rested on the couch. Mom was a huge support and occupied herself with chores around the house.

About 1:00 p.m., the physician assistant from work called and asked what my blood pressure was. I told her it was very high. The OB-GYN doctor in that office said to call my doctor. I did, and he said for me to go to the hospital right away. When Mike came home from work, he drove Mom and me to the hospital.

At 5:00 p.m., I had blood drawn and left a urine sample. A nurse gave me an injection of something which she said would mature the baby's lungs. I was 29 weeks along in my pregnancy, eleven weeks short of full term, which is forty weeks.

A monitor was placed around my abdomen to check the baby's heart rate and my contractions, which were three minutes apart, although I didn't feel them. She explained that with each contraction, my baby's heart rate slowed down. The cervix had already started to dilate to one centimeter out of ten, or full dilation, ready for the baby to come through the birth canal. This was happening way too early. I knew I was in danger, and so was the baby.

The OB-GYN specialist came into my room. He told me that my blood pressure was dangerously high, and my blood platelet level was extremely low at 90,000. He explained that platelets are the clotting factor in the blood, and normally the platelet level in the blood should be about 300,000. My blood was not able to clot very well, which could mean danger of bleeding anywhere in both of us. I needed bed rest, and the doctors and nurses would keep me monitored. Mike and Mom stayed by my side.

Intending to do some Christmas shopping in Minneapolis, my sister and her husband drove from their home in Illinois to St. Paul. When they arrived at our house and discovered we weren't home, she called my aunt who told them that we were at the hospital. Mike left the hospital at 8:45 p.m. to meet my sister and her husband at our house so they could follow him to the hospital.

My family was together and I felt blessed. Only God could have arranged that miracle. Still, I missed my dad.

I asked Mom to call a lady from church to put me on the prayer chain. I also asked Mom to call my co-worker. In the meantime, God assured me of His Presence. I was not to fear, but to trust Him. The words of a song went through my mind:

> Be still and know that I am God.
> I'm right here by your side.
> Be still and find Me there.

Everything looked bleak, and now our health seemed to be in danger. I definitely had preeclampsia, and was glad that I did not have the seizures that accompany eclampsia.

At 9:00 p.m., someone came in and drew more blood, and a half hour later, the obstetrician arrived. He said that the blood sample showed that my platelet level dropped further to 77,000. I had very little clotting factor in my blood and could easily hemorrhage. The baby needed to be delivered very soon. He asked me to call Mike to explain that the baby needed to be delivered, but he would wait until Mike returned.

"Tell him not to speed."

Mike returned with my sister and her husband following behind. God reassured him that He loved our baby even more than we could, and those words comforted him.

I was wheeled into the operating room to prepare for a C-section, Mike sat close to my head, and a blue drape was placed like a curtain so we couldn't see anything below my chest. I grieved to think my pregnancy would be over in minutes.

My doctor gave me an epidural block to numb my body from the waist down. Fear and panic overtook me, and I began to breathe heavily. I turned to Mike for comfort. One nurse noticed what was happening to me and quickly put an oxygen mask over my face to calm me down.

The surgical procedure began. I sensed a slight tugging on the skin in my pelvic area and could hear every word that the doctors, nurses, and anesthesiologist said. I asked Mike to pray for me because I was scared.

My primary doctor slipped into the surgery room to assist. In spite of his being dressed completely in surgical garb, I recognized his glasses.

At 11:03 p.m., only 15 minutes after the procedure began, there was a burst of commotion with fast moving doctors and nurses. I was baffled, because I didn't hear the baby cry. Mike and some of the surgical staff hovered over the small table on the other side of the room, but there was silence. I was confused, and feared the worst. My primary doctor finally said, "Bonnie, you have a little girl."

I heard a squeaky cry, and smiled, relieved that our daughter was alive.

Mike and I talked about baby's names before the procedure began. We came up with either Elizabeth Joy or Krista Joy. We chose Krista Joy, spelled with a "K" because

Mike's niece, Christine, spelled her name with a "C", and we didn't want two cousins in the family with similarly spelled names.

Krista weighed in at two pounds six ounces, and measured nineteen inches long. One of the intensive care nurses held her up for me to see, but his arm was covering her face, so I could only see her tiny, blanket-covered body. Then he whisked her to the newborn intensive care unit (NICU).

As the doctor stapled my incision, he said the placenta, which provides nourishment for the baby through the umbilical cord, had already started to tear away from the inside of the uterus wall, so he was glad that Krista was born when she was.

In the intensive care unit, my blood pressure continued to be high, so the nurse monitored me closely throughout the night. Whenever I moved slightly, the nurse attended to my every need. With all the intravenous tubes, monitor wires, blood pressure cuff, and urine catheter, I couldn't move far. While awake, I remembered that I was now a mother and recalled my doctor's words,

"You have a little girl."

How kind of him to tell me, when everyone else hovered around her, because the moment of her birth was so chaotic.

Meanwhile, Mike joined my mom, sister, and brother-in-law in the hospital waiting room. The two pastors from our new church were also in the waiting area and stayed with my family while Mike was with me in surgery. We had only been at that church for a month, so their kind actions spoke volumes to me about their care and concern.

Sometime during the night I woke up. My immediate thought was, "Breathe, Krista, breathe." I sensed this very intensely and was fearful that she might die. In the morning, I found out that her lung had collapsed, and she needed to be put on a respirator to breathe.

Later, I learned that the entire syndrome I experienced in the last few weeks of my pregnancy was called *HELLP Syndrome*, a form of fulminating, fast-moving preeclampsia. "H" stood for hemolysis, which means that red blood cells in the body are being destroyed. "EL" is for elevated liver enzymes, which indicates that the liver function is abnormal, and "LP" was for low platelets, meaning that the number of platelets, the blood-clotting factors in the blood, were low. Any bleeding was a danger for the baby and me.

The article I read recently on HELLP Syndrome stated that this destructive process only stops with the delivery of the baby. The most common symptom in 90% of women with HELLP Syndrome is upper right-stomach pain with nausea and vomiting. I had experienced severe upper stomach pain and vomiting the night before Krista was born but thought it was from the Swedish meatballs. Even so, it took me several years before I would eat those again!

The syndrome usually comes on before the thirty-sixth week of pregnancy. Severe high blood pressure is seen in half of the cases. In my case, the OB-GYN specialist said it was actually *fulminating* preeclampsia, because it came on so quickly. I had all three symptoms—high blood pressure, protein in the urine, and fluid retention, or edema, in my ankles, hands, and face.

The article went on to say that in some cases convulsions and jaundice can occur, which happens when the liver becomes damaged. There can be gastrointestinal bleeding, blood in the urine from a bleeding urinary tract system, and bleeding from the gums. This bleeding means that the platelet count had dropped. My platelet level dropped radically in four hours, from 5:00 p.m. to 9:00 p.m. that night. As a result, Krista had bleeding within her brain. I still have evidence of tiny red hemorrhage spots scattered across my abdomen from bleeding that started to come through my skin. Krista required blood transfusions after she was born. Praise God, the bleeding in her brain stopped over the next few days as evidenced by a CT scan.

The article on HELLP Syndrome concluded that the name of the syndrome indicated the importance of recognizing it early in the pregnancy because of its association with the high death rate of mother and baby.

I realize now how fragile Krista's life and my life were that night. I had no idea of its seriousness at the time, or I could have fallen into more fear and despair than I did. God was our hope and refuge in the unknown then, and He reassured me in the midst of our crisis. I trusted Him, and knew that He remained by my side.

LETTER TO KRISTA:

THOUGHTS ON PSALM 139
PERSONALIZED FOR KRISTA

Dear Krista,

God created your every part. All your days were ordained by Him. Before you existed, you were in the mind
of God and you are fearfully and wonderfully made.

You were born at 11:03 p.m. on Thursday night, October 27, 1988. In the beginning, your life was fragile. The
doctors and nurses did everything they could to keep you
alive and breathing. Mom and Dad and many others from
around the world were praying for you, Krista. You are a
miracle baby in my eyes. He is a BIG GOD and He loves
you!

Jeremiah 1:5 says, "Before I formed you in the womb, I
knew you." Even after your birth, God continued to form
you, and we witnessed it in many ways.

One of the biggest medical problems you had was with
your lungs. The evening before you were born, the doctor
ordered two injections of medicine for me that helped your
lungs develop. At first, you breathed on your own. However, during the night while you were in the neonatal intensive care unit, a chest x-ray confirmed that one of your
lungs had collapsed. Once again, the doctor and nurses
gathered around you and put a tube down your throat into
your lungs and hooked it up to a respirator to help you
breathe. Before knowing this, I remember waking in the
night and thinking, "Breathe, Krista, breathe," the com-

mand coming from deep inside. I think it was a prayer that He would breathe His life into you.

How hard it was for me to see you the day after your birth with that big tube in your throat, secured with white adhesive taped to your face. I said, "Hi Krista, this is your mom." You tried to cry but couldn't. I cry even thinking about it. I'm sure it hurt a lot, but it kept you alive, Krista.

After six days on the respirator, your lungs became strong enough for you to breathe on your own. We praised God again for sparing your life.

We were informed that the University of Minnesota was conducting a research project. Here, some premature babies, the experimental group, would be given an injection of an artificial substance that acted like surfactant, the slippery liquid around your lungs that allows them to slide and not stick to the rest of your "insides". Some babies were given a placebo, the control group. No one would know until the research was over which baby was given the real surfactant. We were asked if we would like you to be part of the study, so we consented, and you were given the injection. Much later, we were informed that you did not receive the artificial surfactant. God made real surfactant for you and your lungs worked perfectly fine.

At first, your liver wasn't breaking down your red blood cells so your skin started turning yellow. I called the church prayer chain and asked them to pray that God would heal your liver. That day, the nurses put you under ultraviolet lights to help your liver work better. Before you were under those lights, the nurses put a tiny diaper under you, no bigger than a baby doll's diaper! They also put a tiny, two-inch black mask over your eyes, like the one on the main character in the movie, "Zorro," the "masked bandit." After just one day under the lights, your liver worked normally! Your skin wasn't yellow.

God made your red blood cells and platelets multiply quickly. He dried up the bleeding in your brain, so by the next time you had a CT scan, there was no trace of blood.

Even though you were tiny, God helped you grow longer and gain weight quickly. I kept a record of your daily weights, and although you gained only a few ounces each day, you had steady growth.

Your doctor told me that you had a heart murmur, which most likely was caused by a "hole" in your heart. In full term babies this hole has closed. In your case, it wasn't. If it didn't close soon, you would need heart surgery. People from the church prayed that God would close the hole. Wonderfully, He did! You did not need heart surgery after all.

When you were born, the outside of your ears were floppy, with no cartilage to give them shape. When the nurses laid you on your side, your ears stuck to the side of your head. Slowly, God caused cartilage to form in your ears, along with the fingernails and toe nails that you didn't have when you were born. We saw these miracles daily.

God's hand was on you from the very beginning. He knew you would survive those first few days when you struggled so much for breath.

Part of Jeremiah 1:5 says, "Before you were born, I set you apart." God has a wonderful plan for your life, Krista. Satan's plan was to destroy your life, but God's plan far outweighs the enemy's! God set you apart before you were born to fulfill HIS purposes in your life.

Your name, Krista Joy Connolly means, "Joyful follower of Christ, not for herself." I hope and pray that this will be true. We will do our best to raise you in the ways of God, not only by word, but by our actions, too.

Love, Mom

KRISTA'S HOSPITAL STAY

Krista was in the hospital from October 27, to December 23, 1988, a total of 59 days. There were only a few times that I missed the daily trip to see her. My journal contained few entries. Quiet times with the Lord were dry. I rarely cracked open the Bible except on Sundays at church. It was certainly a strange, different time in my life. I was now a mother, but I didn't feel like one with Krista still in the hospital.

My relationship with Mike changed as well. We put our time and energy into daily hospital trips and could only hold our baby once a week on Thursdays, since she was born on a Thursday.

I think back to that time and believe that I had postpartum depression. However, I did not seek help, because my life didn't seem that different from what I had experienced before, with mood changes, and depression. It was a dark and gloomy November and December.

NOVEMBER LETTER TO KRISTA

Dear Krista,

After you were born, you needed to stay in the NICU for eight weeks. However, on Friday, November 4, I was discharged from the hospital after eight days.

I couldn't drive yet, because of my C-section incision. People from church and relatives drove me to the hospital so I could see you. Dad went there during his lunch break from work, and sometimes in the evening with me.

Throughout each day, I collected my milk in plastic jars and took them to the hospital. You received this milk through a tiny tube placed through your nose to your stomach. The tube was attached to a syringe and held above your head until gravity emptied the syringe of milk into your stomach.

When you were six days old on November 1, you could breathe on your own apart from the respirator. Many people from all over the world prayed for you and God healed you of so many things. I am so grateful that He allowed you to live.

Love, Mom

DEDICATION TO THE LORD: LETTER TO KRISTA

Dear Krista,

When you were eight days old on November 3, we dedicated you to the Lord. In the Bible, Luke records that on the eighth day of Jesus' life, Mary and Joseph took Him to the temple and had him dedicated to God. We prayed and agreed to raise you to the best of our ability in the Christian faith.

The next day, we held you for the first time. While we held you closely for thirty minutes, the nurses took a picture of us. After those brief, thirty minutes, you returned to the incubator. We had to wait another week before holding you again, although we put our hands through the portholes of the incubator to touch you.

Love, Mom

LETTER TO KRISTA: MONTH OF DECEMBER

Dear Krista,

On December 1, you weighed three pounds, eleven ounces. Your days were routine in the NICU. You grew steadily on milk, the loving care of the Lord, doctors, nurses, and us. On December 14, you weighed four pounds, nine ounces.

As Christmas drew near, we wondered if you could come home for the holiday. The doctors would only say that you were doing well. Originally, we were told that you could come home on your due date, which was January 8.

Unexpectedly, on December 21, the doctor announced that we could take you home the next day, in less than twenty-four hours. Finally, we talked the doctors into having you stay a couple more days so we could make our home ready and buy what we needed for you.

We arranged to stay with you in the board and care hospital room for December 22 and December 23. During the drive to the hospital that morning, I meditated on the first Christmas when Jesus was born. Mary had to feed, change, and burp Him. God entrusted Mary, a young girl of fourteen or sixteen years old, to be His mother. He was born in a stable, yet I was worried if your nursery would be good enough. We hadn't finished painting your room, so we placed your cradle in the living room. Jesus' mother didn't have to worry how long it took paint to dry, but she certainly had to trust God. Proverbs 3:5-6 says, "Trust in the Lord with all your heart and lean not on your own understanding; in all your ways submit to him, and he will make your paths straight," a promise that holds true today.

On the drive to the hospital, God said to me:

I have prepared you for this.

While "rooming in" with you, I tried to nurse you, but that proved difficult for us. During the night, you woke up frequently, and so did I, with each sound you made. Yet, they were the wonderful sounds of our first child, a very precious gift from God.

Love, Mom

LETTER TO KRISTA: YOUR FIRST CHRISTMAS

Dear Krista,

On Christmas Day, I stayed home with you while your dad went to church. My parents, and an aunt and uncle came with dinner so we could celebrate our first Christmas together.

For the first few days you were home, I became overwhelmed with the responsibility of caring for you. I worried about making mistakes. Other thoughts troubled me such as, "I don't know how to be a mother." Finally, I prayed, "Lord, this is too difficult for me. I need Your help."

I wanted to do a good job of being your mother that my role began to seem overwhelming. What I really meant to pray was, "God take away the stresses and source of struggle in my life."

Soon after I prayed, I caught a glimpse of God's purposes for you,

Krista is a person who has a part in My master plan. Raise her for My glory. Meet her physical needs now. Instill in her eternal values.

Then I remembered the words the Lord encouraged me with the day I left for the hospital to room in with you when He said,

Bonnie, I have prepared you for this.

Love, Mom

A NEW YEAR BEGINS

On January 7, 1989, Krista was ten weeks old. The Lord spoke these words:

The key is to think of caring for Krista as an act of service to Me. She is a person of eternal value to Me. She has a body that needs physical attention and care until she is old enough to care for herself. She has a body that houses a soul which has eternal value, created by and for Me. Instill in her My values. May she remember her parents as ones who possess My nature, with My fruit of love, patience, and gentleness.

God made Krista, and she is His, a precious newborn lamb in His pasture.

HOME FROM THE HOSPITAL

Early days at home with Krista seemed like a blur. She continued to grow slowly, and I became more comfortable as I developed a routine. My moments of relaxation came when Krista slept, and most often I fell into bed exhausted, only to wake two or three hours later to feed her.

At the end of January, when Krista was three months old, there was a turning point in my life and walk with the Lord. I received a cassette tape from a pediatrician friend in Haiti. She recorded encouraging words with sound advice and recommended that I have quiet times again with God. I followed her advice.

I asked the Lord for direction, and He gave me a strategy. I read the Book of Psalms backwards, starting with Psalm 150, which focused on praising God. He also directed me to read Proverbs, beginning with the first chapter.

Daily time in God's word helped tremendously to get back on track. I also learned to depend on others and cry out for help when needed.

On February 8, I wrote, "By God's word, sustaining all things, and all my righteousness in Him, I stand complete in Him." I was on my way toward emotional, physical, and spiritual health, and I was so grateful for my friend's prodding to read God's word daily. I had no idea this could make such a drastic difference in how I lived my daily life with Mike and Krista, but it certainly did.

GIVING UP MY RIGHTS

During February and March, my journal entries described discouragement, despair, and frustration. I gave up my personal rights to take a shower, have a quiet time, eat, or sleep when I wanted. I couldn't always have clean clothes when I wished if Krista threw up on them. However, Mike often helped with a needed heart lift, and the Lord reminded me of things I could do.

Psalm 131:1-2 says, "But I have calmed and quieted myself, I am like a weaned child with its mother; like a weaned child I am content." The verse reminded me of Krista. After nursing, she slept with a smile while milk remained on her lips and cheek. Her arms went limp as in a deep, restful sleep. My soul was to be still and quiet like hers.

MY GRACE IS SUFFICIENT

On March 3, I experienced much frustration. The adjustments to Krista's schedule continued. I started listing one difficulty after the next to myself:

- *That day, a seminar on depression was being given by a nurse's organization. I wanted to go, but I had no car.*

- *There was a blizzard outside.*

- *Krista threw up twice—once after her bath all over her clean clothes, body, and me. The other time was after my shower, when she threw up all over herself, my clean clothes and body.*

- *In case I found a ride to the seminar, I looked for my breast pump equipment in Krista's box of clothes but I couldn't find one part I needed.*

Krista watched my frenzied actions from her swing and looked as if she wondered what was up with me. When I picked her up to cuddle her, she smiled and laughed. That made me laugh, and her eyes got big.

I found it was possible to have a sense of humor about such things. "A cheerful heart is good medicine, but a crushed spirit dries up the bones (Proverbs 17:22).

Daniel had no way out of the lion's den. Shadrach, Meshach, and Abednego found no way out of the fiery furnace. Then, God spoke,

My grace is sufficient for you.

Nothing changed in my outward circumstance, and I did not go to the seminar. Yet, I no longer felt trapped. He lifted the heaviness and gave me joy. I prayed for an attitude change, and He gave me new hope. I praised the Lord and experienced His grace.

DIRECTION FOR THIS TIME IN LIFE

I asked God for clarity, and I believe God gave His perspective, direction, and focus to my life:

1. *I am called to be a follower, friend, and lover of Jesus, and to have a deep, relationship with Him with constant, two-way communication.*

2. *As Mike's wife, I am to love him, be his intimate friend and confidant, be submissive, and keep a peaceful home for Mike and Krista.*

3. *I am the only mother Krista will have. This is a high calling. I am to nurture her with love, meet her physical*

needs, and promote an atmosphere of security, love, and protection.

4. *I am to eat well, obtain proper rest, and stay healthy to provide adequate breast milk for her nutritional needs.*

5. *I am to improve homemaking skills and promote an atmosphere of peace and rest in our home.*

6. *God has called us to be a part of a local church. I am to play the piano skillfully during worship and follow the guidelines given by the music director.*

7. *God gave me a heart for missions, and I am to pray and support them as He leads.*

8. *I am to ask God for opportunities to serve my neighbors and pray for them.*

9. *I am to maintain a good relationship with relatives and ask God to show me when to spend time with them.*

10. *I am to correspond with friends by letter and phone calls as the Holy Spirit leads.*

11. *I am to listen to the Holy Spirit each minute of the day, ready to be obedient to His promptings and have a fulfilling sense of perfect timing throughout the day.*

HEAVENLY HOMEMAKING

Krista was five months old. Caring for her became routine, yet keeping up with house work was difficult. I reviewed a Bible study guide about homemaking, which became a turning point for me in taking responsibility for home maintenance and caring for children.

Part of the Bible study that stood out to me was based on Titus 2:3-5. I found the following principles for women:

1. *Teach older women to be reverent in the way they live.*

2. *They are not to be slanderers.*

3. *They are not to be addicted to wine.*

4. *Teach what is good.*

5. *Train younger women to love their husbands and children.*

6. *Be self-controlled, pure, busy at home, kind, and good natured.*

7. *Be subject to, obedient to, and adapted to your husband.*

8. *Do not to malign the word of God.*

I wanted our home to be a sweet resting place and refuge for Mike, Krista, and anyone else who came. My goals toward homemaking were based on many scriptures I found which gave me God's perspective on homework and my priorities:

- *Proverbs 31:27 states, "She watches over the affairs of her household and does not eat the bread of idleness."*

- *1 Corinthians 10:31 states, "So whether you eat or drink or whatever you do, do it all for the glory of God."*

- *"And whatever you do, whether in word or deed, do it all in the name of the Lord Jesus, giving thanks to God the Father through him (Colossians 3:17).*

- *"Whatever you do, work at it with all your heart, as working for the Lord, not for human masters, since you know that you will receive an inheritance from the Lord as a reward. It is the Lord Christ you are serving (Colossians 3:23).*

- *Be thankful for having a home to keep up. My desire and will is to be thankful for the home God provided for us (1 Thessalonians 5:18).*

- *Have the same mind and attitude as Jesus when He washed the disciple's feet. He told them to wash others' feet—that is, be a servant to them, too. He encouraged them to follow His example by serving others. This is the path of blessing (John 13:12-17).*

- *Be known for your good deeds. Bring up your children well, show hospitality, wash the feet of the saints, relieve the suffering of the afflicted, and devote yourself to do good in every way (1 Timothy 5:9-10).*

YOU ARE MY CHILDREN

Frustration about raising Krista again overwhelmed me on April 7. My prayer was, "Lord, I would like to talk with someone, but who? Surely You never had children to know what it is like as a parent." God's response was:

Yes I do. All of you are My children and want to go your own way, yet I am patient and gentle. I still love you.

"Lord, teach me how to be patient and gentle with Krista at times when I'm at the end of my rope. Sometimes I don't have patience, kindness and gentleness. I know that the way I react is not right. Krista demands my attention every minute she is awake, and when I don't have time alone with Mike, I speak harshly to her. She doesn't know any better and is helplessly dependent on us for her care. Show me what is right."

Two days later, I listened to a teaching about abandonment to the Lord. The speaker said, "When our will crosses God's, we need to just give up."

I prayed, "I give up my will for Yours, Lord."

A few days later, another key came back to mind. The Lord had impressed on me concerning care for Krista:

I have prepared you for this.

When I worked at a cardiac intensive care unit in 1978, I asked, "Lord, why am I here? I don't like this job." As I looked back, I understood that God worked perseverance in me during stressful times, which helped prepare me to care for Krista.

YOU ARE CLEAN

In late April, after I rocked Krista and placed her in her crib, the Lord enveloped me in His Presence and said,

You are clean.

This theme, "You are clean," repeated itself to me over the next few days, until I had a quiet time with the Lord. He showed me insecurities that ran deep:

Don't bring up former sins. I covered you with My blood on Calvary. You are washed white as snow. Don't let the tempter tell you otherwise. I'm pronouncing you worthy in My eyes. You are precious in My sight no matter what others think.

I'm exposing the roots of insecurity which goes back to childhood. I want to expose the roots for what they are. I will show you in your mind how they began. Listen to me now. You may feel naked and exposed. Your fleshly defenses are being pulled down, but I will clothe you with My defenses. They stand the wind and weather of life far better than the defenses that you have built yourself and those the father of lies has built around you. They will only stand as a barrier between you and other people. The derelicts and shipwrecks, who are down and out, will come. You will see their coat of defenses. I will allow you to see their hearts once I've changed you and given you My new coat of arms to wear.

Put on your robe of righteousness. Clothe your mind against the attacks of the enemy that try to wear you down with old thoughts. I will free you from your old thought patterns. Remember, I am gentle and will only do what is best for you.

What I have to offer is something better and more lasting than what the world gives. Don't worry about all that went on inside of you yesterday when you and Mike met with your pastor. It matters that you prayed, even though you

didn't want to. Part of the root began growing deep in your childhood. You've kept it hidden it deep inside, so you didn't even recognize when you were hurt, because you buried the hurt so quickly. Remember how quickly your mom wanted to forget the confrontation? You buried anything that angered you in your childhood and wanted to be known as a good child who spoke little and never angered.

Many times your anger came because you were hurt. I will show you better ways of coping with your anger. Let Me show you the root cause of your anger, and let Me show you My way. Allow Me to help you work through memories.

Let this word settle as dust settles on the ground, even in times of anger. You will be able to see more clearly. Times of adversity will come, but they will teach you My ways and break the old patterns of thought. I long for you to rest in Me, which is easier than you think. Hide yourself in Me. Run to Me when you are overwhelmed. Don't try to hide your sins again when they are exposed. Confess, and let Me cleanse them or show you if it is a lie. I will teach you the difference.

Regarding others, they are responsible to Me for their sins. If you point out their sin, they may feel naked and only want to run and hide from you. Instead, show them the cloak of righteousness and love they can have as they trust in Me as Savior and Lord. Tell them how much I love them. I created them to be whole, untarnished vessels, polished for use in My Kingdom.

I will give you words to say. You will know My words because the sense of condemnation and panic will not be there. Rest and trust Me. I will never deceive you. I came that you may be whole and have abundant life. You have more power when you are clothed and hidden in Me. I give you the keys to My Kingdom. Enter in and find rest where I am King.

Two songs came to mind, "I Will Put on My Robe of Righteousness," and "O Lord Your Tenderness," especially the words about His tenderness that melt all our bitterness, and receiving His love which changes our ugliness.

The Lord also sensed my desire to return to Hawaii and He said,

> *I'll take you to Hawaii when it will be easiest for you and Krista—not now. I need to have you see the difference between her cries of hunger and sleep. Feed her with solid food, so she is more satisfied in public places. The Psalm for today will bless you!*

This day I read Psalm 85 and made comments:

"You showed favor to Your land, Lord."

I thought of my own "land" which signified my body, and how it was meant to be treated.

"You restored the fortunes of Jacob."

God restored the parts of me that were tarnished during my rebellious years. I had searched for love in relationships that did not fulfill me.

"You forgave the iniquity of Your people and covered all their sins."

He forgave me. He covered my past sins and made me as clean as freshly fallen snow."

"You set aside Your entire wrath and turned from Your fierce anger."

> *I am restoring you. I am God, Your Savior. I have put away My displeasure towards you. I will not prolong My anger through all your generations and offspring. I will receive you again, and You will rejoice in Me. I will show you My unfailing love, Bonnie. I promised you peace. I will not let you return to your folly. Surely My salvation is near to you. Bonnie, I know you fear Me. My glory will dwell in you.*

Right now, your love and faithfulness for Mike and his love and faithfulness for you, will meet together. I will restore your oneness. TOGETHER you will shine with My glory. Take off the old, tattered garment of gloom about your relationship with Mike. I am giving you a new garment, a new robe of righteousness, peace, and love. Put it around both of you. The relationship will be new in your private time. The fruit of your union will be evident to all, and My glory will shine like a dove above you. Your relationship will bring glory to Me. I love you and will complete the work I began ten years ago and even in eternity.

I chose you together to be My vessels even before one day came to be. I love you, and will never leave you to fight this battle alone. It will be a climb, but the feasting on the fruit of it will be worth it in the end. Don't fear the heights. You will not fall. Keep your eyes on top of the mountain, not on the depths below, or you will surely lose your balance and fall. The depths below are your past sins. Focusing on them will only bring you down. Don't forget the victories and forgiveness, because I brought you through. This is a time of victory. I will do new things ahead.

Psalm 85:10 says, "Love and faithfulness meet together; righteousness and peace kiss each other."

Just as in the righteous robe of marriage.

Psalm 85:11 says, "Faithfulness springs forth from the earth, and righteousness looks down from heaven."

Faithfulness will spring forth from you too, Bonnie. You need never fear that you will walk out on Mike. I will keep you together. Turn always to Me. I will indeed give what is good.

Psalm 85:12 says, "Your land will yield its harvest."

You will conceive again. This will be the fruit, your reward for living within the confinement of My righteousness. It may seem a narrow space at times, but oh, so freeing to you when you walk in My ways. Your steps will seem sure and steady. How I long to teach you of this narrow way. The key will be to be led by My voice. I will be there saying, "This is the way. Walk in it.

Psalm 85:13 says, "Righteousness goes before your way and prepares the way for your steps."

ON EMOTIONS

EXPOSING THE ROOTS OF THE PAST

Sunday April 30, 1989, was the day of Krista's dedication at church. In the afternoon, I took a nap. When I woke up, my thoughts turned to my Mom and Dad. Perhaps Mom had difficulty in raising us, while Dad worked many hours of overtime and spent most evenings in the basement watching TV. Did I sense rejection?

I prayed, "Lord, I choose to forgive Dad for the times I thought he rejected me." God helped me with thoughts of rejection and said:

> Let Me expose the root of rejection. I will show you the root of bitterness, rejection, criticism, and anger so you can heal. I do the healing. Freedom and joy will be the fruits, not guilt, condemnation, or depression.

God brought the truth. Dad hadn't been in the basement all the time, as I had thought. I remembered wrongly. "I love you, Dad."

Frustration and depression were paramount in May. Krista turned six months old. I cried out and asked God for His perspective:

> I am doing a perfect work in you. Do not fret over the emotions that flood your mind. I am teaching you how to channel these emotions in My way of righteousness. I will restore balance to your emotions. I will bring you through this period of darkness so you only remember the lasting work which I have done.

Focus not on the overwhelming sea of emotions. Instead, look to the Rock of your salvation, Christ, who sits at the right hand of the Father, making intercession for you. I will never leave or forsake you, though at times, it may seem as if I have turned away My face.

The road I have chosen for you is not easy, but will produce lasting results. If others do not follow Me, love them just the same. Lay down your judgment. Choose understanding, compassion, and love for those who may seem blind to you. I am their judge. I know their motives and understand their hearts. Love them into My way of righteousness.

MARRIAGE PARTNER

A sea of emotions overwhelmed me and I turned to the Lord for answers. He knew my thoughts and replied,

Look at Mike as a person, not as a marriage partner. Do not get caught up in marriage as an institution or say, 'Our marriage stinks'.

I asked the Lord why I felt insecure, had a sense of unworthiness, and did not feel important. I knew of someone who married an older man so he could provide, as her alcoholic father had not.

I thought of my dad, and never feared that he would fail to financially provide for our family. Growing up, I always thought we had money for our needs and wants. I had the impression that Dad always had cash in his billfold. Mom was frugal to a point, but we often had treats and home-made goodies.

Now, we hardly had enough money to make ends meet, and needed to watch every penny. As a child, I felt more secure. Now, I have more questions than answers. Finally, God assured me that He provides what we need and urged me to be content with what we had.

IMPATIENCE

When Mike returned from a business trip in Bemidji, Minnesota, he wanted to unload his car. On the contrary, I wanted to talk with him first and I grew impatient. After caring for Krista while she was sick with pneumonia, I was exhausted. When I questioned the Lord about my frustration, He gave me insight the next day:

You needed Mike's support last night when he returned home. He wanted to unload the car, but you thought it would take too long and became impatient. It took him five minutes at the most. You assumed that he did not care for you or want to spend time with you at a time of crisis during Krista's illness. At a time when the atmosphere for his homecoming should have been peaceful, it was chaotic. A satanic attack began ten minutes before Mike walked into the house. He can easily become unglued when the house is messy.

After discussing all that had transpired while Mike was away, we forgave each other. The next day we drove to Rochester for a wedding, and while Mike stayed to visit his family, I drove with my parents back to our house. Mom and Dad dropped Krista and me at our home, and then drove another four hours to theirs.

Dad called me at 6:00 p.m. that evening and said that Mom had suffered a stroke. She had temporary paralysis and slurred speech, yet, was able to talk with me briefly on the phone. This seemed too much for me to take. I called Mike's parents, and they said that Mike was on his way and should be home shortly.

I needed to draw strength from the Lord and lean on Him. Encouragement came as I read in Joshua 1:5-9 (NLT), "No one will be able to stand against you as long as you live. For I will be with you as I was with Moses. I will not fail you or abandon you. Be strong and courageous. Do not be afraid or discouraged. For the LORD your God is with you wherever you go."

Nothing had changed outwardly, but I felt lighter, and was filled with God's inner strength to face whatever came next.

While being mother to seven-month old Krista, I sometimes felt overwhelmed with my commitment as pianist at church. I called four women and asked what their church involvement had been when their children were young. Although each had a different answer, they prayed and encouraged me. God responded:

I have called you to be a mother to Krista. Be an expression of love to her from Me. Show her My love and care, and you will find contentment. I have called you to be a mom, a nursing mom's support group leader, wife to Mike, and a servant to your mother. Be an expression of Me in whatever position, place, or relationship you have.

PREPARING FOR A TRIP UP NORTH

In June, we spent five days at my parents' home in northern Minnesota. I prayed before we left, and these are the words I held onto from the Lord:

Use self-control with your tongue. Have no thought as to how your parents respond to you. You are responsible to Me for your every thought, motive, deed, and word. Obey Me, and I will give you moment by moment instructions. Meditate on My word, and I will be faithful to make it come alive in you and be a part of you.

GIFT GIVING

Krista was nine months old in August. I took her shopping for Mike's anniversary gift. I bought him a book that I thought he might enjoy. On our tenth anniversary, he stayed up half the night reading it, and I became frustrated. "Lord, help me see Your perspective on my frustrations." He said:

You became angry at Mike for being enthralled in that book you gave him as an anniversary present. What was the source of your frustration? Was it not that he sought the gift and seemed so delighted in the gift that he forgot the giver? Wasn't it that you felt neglected and rejected because the book seemed to satisfy him more than you, the book's giver? When he stayed up until 2:00 a.m. reading that book, delighting in the gift, instead of in you, did you feel hurt and rejected? You said, "What must I do to gain his attention and affection again?"

Seek Me and be found by Me. Give gifts without expecting people to shower you with love and attention, saying, "Aren't you wonderful because you are such a great gift-giver. You have worth."

A true gift will produce delight. Let that be your reward for giving, that the attention be rightly on the gift to give the other person pleasure. Your gift delighted the person you intended to bless. Your reward will be in heaven. Do not expect rewards from people, even from Mike. Do not expect him to drop the gift and be enthralled with you. It may never happen. Rejoice in Me, who gave you the idea for the gift. You were the vessel through whom I chose to bless him.

Give your feelings of rejection to Me. I love you and will never reject you the way you perceived that Mike rejected you or how you perceive other people reject you when they don't call, write, or visit.

Be assured of My love for you. You are precious in My sight. You are special. I wrap My arms around you and desire an intimate relationship with you. It is this union of soul that You are longing for, but it can only be found in Me. I am the Giver of all that you have. Do not reject Me as a Giver and only look at the gift that I give. You will never be completely satisfied with the gifts. Instead, look to Me, the Giver of gifts, which are beyond the gifts and treasures of this world, even beyond the treasures of Mike, Krista, your special friends, and relationships on this earth. As you depend only on these other relationships to fill you, it will seem as if you have holes in your pocket through which all your treasures fall out to be lost forever. I am that treasure. Store up treasures in heaven.

DIRECTION YOU SEEK

In late August, God heard my cry about being a mother to Krista. He said,

As for the direction you seek for every decision, fear not that you will miss the way I have chosen. You will not find happiness in external things, places, or relationships. I give you them to enjoy for a season, but hold onto them loosely. Your treasures will be in heaven.

I will bring teachers who will instruct you on how to care for Krista. Your main concern is that she is not growing adequately or is not getting the nutrients that she needs to sustain her. Her rate of growth is slower than you expected, and this is the cause of your frustration. The nutritionist will give you some guidelines, but remember that she does not have all the answers. Let Me define the problem areas, and then I will lead you in the path that I wish for you regarding her growth and development in spiritual, physical, and emotional needs. She is My child and creation. You are a good mom. You care deeply that she be well fed, and dressed properly for warmth or cold, and these are valid needs.

I clothe the lilies of the field. I feed the birds of the air, even in the wintertime when food is scarce. I will see to it that your baby gets the food she needs to sustain her, and cause good growth in her. Leave the growing to Me. Provide the right environment for her to flourish, and I will bring the right kind and amount of growth for her. Leave that burden to Me.

Rest in Me. You will hear My voice behind you, whether it be to the left or to the right. You will hear Me say, "This is the way. Walk in it." You will be led and guided by the peace in your heart. I love you and will not lead you astray. Krista belongs to Me and you are her mother. This is true; yet, I have full responsibility for her life.

MORE PRECIOUS THAN RUBIES

In late September, we visited our friends in northern Minnesota. During a prayer time with them, the Lord spoke these words to me,

You are more precious than rubies. Somehow, your sense of rejection as a child was mixed in with a sense of worthlessness. If someone rejected you, you felt that you must not be worthy of their attention, but you, My child, are more precious than rubies.

My friend had these words for me, which I believe were from the Lord,

Be perfect. You are being made perfect. You do not have to be perfect.

She had a picture of Jesus as an egg-like vessel or capsule. Jesus had the door open, beckoning me to come inside of Him. Once inside with the door closed, I became enclosed in Christ by His Holy Spirit. I am perfect because I entered the door to be enclosed in Him. This is the "perfect me" God sees inside of Jesus. Then, while inside, the work of the Holy Spirit in me continues through trials and inner changing. This is what my friend meant by, "You do not have to be perfect." But, I am being made perfect. This is the working of the Holy Spirit power, the same power that raised Christ from the dead. He quickens my mortal body. This is the process of sanctification. A song came to mind with the words, "The Lord is building Jerusalem," and He is restoring me. He is restoring Zion!

COMPARISON TO OTHERS

In September, I listened to a radio program about a missionary. I prayed, "Lord, there is heaviness in my spirit and emotions today. Why? Show me the root." He encouraged me by these words:

You felt as if you could never have the same love and devotion to Me as that missionary. Only I know your heart and motives. You try to be spiritual for Me, but beyond that, I see a heart of love and devotion that pleases Me. You would choose Me even if all the valuables in your life were burned away. I do not need to test you on that. I know that your heart is focused on Me.

Your gifts and talents are different from hers but not less important, and that is why I have chosen to do a different work in you. I am changing your heart. When I have completed that which I intend, I will cause you to shine forth My glory, in an even greater way.

Others will come to you and wonder what is so different about you. You will then have opportunities to point them to Me, the cause of the true glory and joy that shine within you. You are impatient with My speed, but know that My work in you is lasting and deep. It goes beyond the fuller's brush[3] to reach the very depths of your being to cleanse you and remove all roots of bitterness, pride, and anger. I do a perfect work. Your role is to watch and wait. I will turn your sadness into joy forevermore.

---

3 A fuller was the individual who would take the raw, filthy wool from sheep and purify it using a variety of techniques, including an extremely harsh soap and brush that would ultimately help to make it clean. https://www.biblestudytools.com/dictionary/fuller/. See also Malachi 3:2, KJV, and Mark 9:3. KJV.

CONCERNS

ANOTHER SURPRISE

At the end of September, I went to the clinic because I had missed a period and was extremely tired. My pregnancy test proved positive! I was amazed that I was with child again so quickly. Krista was only nine months old. When I spoke to the Lord about it, He said:

> *Your tiredness and fatigue will pass. As the child within slows down in growth, you will start to pick up energy. For now, the child is growing rapidly, and this requires rest and fuel or food from you. I will tell you when to go and when to rest. It may seem "unspiritual" in the natural, but My eyes see the hidden child that I am forming in your womb, and it will be brought forth as gold, a treasure fit for the Master's use. You will be pleased when you see this gift.*

> *The time of preparation for this child is short. Use your time wisely. Ask Me for wisdom, and I will direct your path and make it smooth. Do not be afraid to say, "No," if it is My "no" for you, because then it needs no further explanation. You are made to expend only the effort I intend for you at this time. You can experience fatigue quickly. Listen to My voice within for every decision ahead, and I will not guide you astray. Krista also needs rest at this time while she is healing from pneumonia.*

CONCERNS ABOUT KRISTA

Krista was almost a year old on October 20. I took notes from a book about being a mother. The book greatly impressed me with its positive outlook on the importance of mothering and nurturing small children. I had some difficulty at this point in my life with Krista's seemingly constant demands. I was concerned that she was as small as she was and still nursing frequently. Also, being pregnant with our second child took a lot of my energy. God's encouraging words came to me:

Do not reject Krista at times like these when she seems so insecure. These memories are leaving a lasting imprint on her. You are with her most of the day. She trusts you. If you ignore her need for attention at this time, she does not know who else to turn to, and she becomes confused and frightened.

You fulfill a very important part in her life right now. I will give you grace to hang in there during the rough times. Later, once she is settled, you will find the rest you need. She wants and needs you. Do not deprive her of this vital love, care, and nurture. Ask Me what to do during the times like you experienced yesterday, and I will clearly answer. Listen for My words within you for what direction and action to take for Krista. I created her and am using you to mold and shape her into what I want her to be. She is a unique child.

Books and other people have advice. I will open your eyes and ears to what I want you to glean from them. My voice will give the final answer. Have confidence in your ability to hear My voice. Choose advice according to My leading. It is easier than you think. Draw close to Me. I want to be your counselor and friend. As you do this, I will add others to your life who will be friends and counselors, but not until I have your assurance that they will not replace Me. I am a jealous God.

RELATING TO RELATIVES

On October 22, I visited my aunt in the hospital. Her son and daughter-in-law were there with their two children. I prayed, "Lord, I have known some of these relatives all my life. Help me be Your instrument to carry Your truth and healing."

In response, I heard:

> You have to lay groundwork first. In building a house, the land first has to be cleared of old rubble, poor foundation, broken glass, and debris. In some cases, the house and land may look perfectly good, yet on the inside, the owner is sad, discontented, or sick. Some may not know where to go for help.

> Seek Me for each of your relatives. I have created them and know their bondages. Only I can set them free. I desire to use you to point them to Me. I am their Master Physician and the Builder of the new foundation and house that they would live in if they choose. I have a place for them in My kingdom. Their false ideas of who I am have caused them to turn their back on Me. They are hungry for truth and love. Show them My way. Introduce them to Me.

> I know your fear of saying the wrong words, but I want you to step out. Open your mouth and I will fill it with My words. Be like Joshua in scripture. Pattern your life after Joshua. I will pave the way before you and I will be with you wherever you go.

This word was an encouragement to me. I had a desire to show my relatives the true nature and character of God, so they could replace the false picture they may have of God. Also, I realized that I might be the only Bible they would ever read.

"Show me the way, Lord. Shine through me today."

AM I DOING ANYTHING FOR YOU, GOD?

In November I prayed, "God, I don't believe I am doing anything for You. I think of people I should call or write, but I don't do anything." God responded:

You are doing something for Me. You are carrying a child. This small baby in your womb belongs to Me. Satan would like to destroy this special child, but I have given it life. Rest often. Be sensitive to the leading of My Spirit. This time is short but crucial. Do all that you know to ensure the best outcome for this pregnancy. I love you and this child. I will bring fellowship to you in times of need. I will tell you what to do by My Spirit. Don't be afraid that you are missing My plan. I will make it clear to you.

I am pleased with you. I will instruct you and teach you which way to go. Mike will follow My plan. Together you will serve Me in a place of My choosing, but that time is not yet. Bloom where you are planted. By My will I planted you in this home, neighborhood, and church. Use what I have given you. Give what I have given you. It will come naturally to you. Trust in Me. Remember the boy in a Viet-Nam orphanage who gave his blood to someone he did not know, even though he thought that he, himself, would die? My love for you is unconditional. I died for you. My blood was poured out for you that you may live and have My newness in you.

RIGHT PATHS

After Christmas, we took Krista to an eye doctor because her eyes were still crossed. I read that if the eyes are still crossed by the time the child reaches six months, surgery may be needed. We took her to an eye doctor who specialized in children, yet we were dissatisfied with the specialist that our insurance would cover. We would have to pay out of pocket to have the surgeon of our choice for Krista's surgery.

I was in turmoil about the situation that morning until I read Psalm 16:11, "You have made known to me that path of life. You fill me with joy in Your Presence, with eternal pleasures at your right hand." Next, I turned to Psalm 9:10,

"For you Lord, have never forsaken those who seek You."
The Lord said:

> *I will not forsake you, or Krista. I created her and know what is best for her. The surgery will be in My time and I will watch over and guard her from all harm. Continue to trust Me. I won't lead you astray. I will not allow you to make a mistake.*

LARK OR NIGHTENGALE

One early morning, while reading in, Streams in the Desert by Mrs. Charles E. Cowman about larks and nightingale birds, I was impressed with a passage about larks and nightingales.[4] The lark was up early with a song. The nightingale sang late in the evening. The comparison was between people who were up early to pray, and those who prayed in the evening. The Lord spoke:

> *There are no spiritual brownie points for being a lark! Remember that, when you are tempted to judge Mike for not having a quiet time in the morning. Besides, it is also hard for you to get up sometimes when I call you to join Me in the morning!*

I was lovingly put in my place!

LIFT UP YOUR HANDS

The house was quiet on January 9. This was the day that I planned to play piano for worship at a Women's Aglow meeting. God impressed on me these words,

> *Look at the words of the songs that you chose for the Women's Aglow meeting today. There is a message in them for you.*

---

[4] Mrs. Charles E. Cowman, Streams in the Desert-1 (Grand Rapids, Michigan: Zondervan Publishing House, 1965), 259, Devotion for August 19.

Some words began standing out to me as I looked over the songs. The time I spent looking over the words set me free. The Lord said,

Things will look so different when you learn to spiritually fly. Use both your wings of prayer and praise. Pray for people you are concerned about and praise Me. Look at your circumstances from My point of view. Ask Me for the whole picture.

The words from one song were, "Praise the Lord... Shake off those heavy bands. Lift up those holy hands again. Praise the Lord when you are down about it. Shake off the heaviness. Lift your hands and praise the Lord."

Words to another song were: "Put on the garment of praise for the spirit of heaviness." When I sense heaviness in my spirit, I can put on praise. I can lift up my voice to God, in other words, talk to Him. I can praise in the Spirit and with understanding. Both are needed.

I want to set you free from your way of thinking toward your relatives. You have hands that hang down with discouragement. Lift up your voice to Me.

"Lord, I am more focused on what I am going to share today, and I'm not allowing You to speak to me. Forgive me, Lord. You alone know about these issues. When I sense Your Presence, Lord, I want to praise and worship You. As I magnify You, Lord, then my problem will seem so insignificant and small in the light of Your glory and grace."

The words to other comforting songs came, "Turn your eyes upon Jesus. Look full in His wonderful face. And the things of earth will grow strangely dim in the light of His glory and grace." And, "Praise to the Lord the Almighty the King of creation! O my soul, praise Him, for He is thy health and salvation!"

He does rule and reign over my situation. He is above it all.

Someone may ask, "How are you doing?"

Sometimes a person may answer, "Fine—under the circumstances."

The Lord's question is, "What are you doing there under your circumstances?"

In my journal, these words came to me. Though I didn't hear this prophetically, I felt the Lord taught me His perspective:

> God is not under the circumstances. He is on top of them. Rise up. Ask Him to show you things as He sees them, and ask Him to give you your needed change of heart, that godly attitude of love and understanding that He has for the people involved. Lift them up to the Lord in prayer. Receive God's love and understanding for them. God will intervene when you allow Him to work in their lives, and you will see the Holy Spirit do the work in them and in you.

> Be responsible to God for your attitudes. Remember, change in you does not come about by your own willpower but by the divine intervention of God. The needed patience, love, understanding, and endurance only come by supernatural intervention of God. We cannot muster this up by our own strength or willpower. He will work in us to change our ways of thinking and to give us each a helmet of salvation.

> Come out from under your tortoise shell. Do not be afraid. Your old ways of thinking are a hard shell around you like a tortoise's shell. Leave old ways of thinking and allow God to put His new helmet on your mind that will withstand and repel the fiery darts of your enemy that target your mind.

> The helmet of salvation will be there for protection. You may sense the darts coming, but the thoughts the enemy would place there such as discouragement, depression, and a

despairing "no way out" mentality, will fall to the ground. If these are the nature of your thoughts, they are not from the Lord. Shake them off. You will get to the place of recognizing more clearly that the source of these thoughts is not from the Lord. He will do the work in you. The fiery darts will fall to the ground and not penetrate your heart and soul to produce the discouragement, depression, despair, and distress Satan would like to see. Do not try to do this on your own.

Come to the Lord. He is your protection and shield. Run to Him. Put out an "SOS" prayer to Him, and He will quickly come to your rescue. Psalm 18:6 says, "In my distress, I called to my God for help. From His temple, He heard my voice. My cry came before Him into His ears." Verse 14 reads, "He shot His arrows and scattered His enemies." Verse 17 says, "He rescued me from my powerful enemy, from my foes who were too strong for me. Verse 18 continues, "They confronted me in the day of my disaster. But the Lord was my support. Verse 19 says, "He brought me out into a spacious place. He rescued me because He delighted in me."

I read Psalm 18 as the Lord directed me, and I reread portions of Catherine Marshall's book, *Light in My Present Darkness*. I felt that the Lord wanted me to observe something in this book that I had read earlier. I turned to the page where Catherine wrote what God had impressed on her, and it echoes what the Lord was speaking to me:

"You are My beloved child, [Bonnie]. Rest in that love. Simply rest in it. Bathe in it. Stop asking so many questions. Stop this probing, taking your spiritual temperature saying, 'Does the Lord want me to do this or do that? Is this right? Is that right?' This is the source of the confusion. You are My child, My disciple. I accepted you long ago as you are, as you are growing. Nothing is between us. Grasp that by faith and all else will follow. Nervous probing is Satan's tactic to

unsettle you, confuse you, and knock you off the base of your belief.

Let My joy flow through you, even though you do not sense any at first. Let it flow, and don't be afraid. My joy will sweep away your fear and uncertainties. Stop accusing yourself, [Bonnie]. Turn any such thoughts over to Me instantly. They come from Satan, not from Me. Place yourself in My hands as though you were an infant. Let Me handle your questions, the tattered remnants of your unbelief, your growth in My grace, not My stringency. I came not to judge or condemn. All accusations come from the enemy. Open the floodgates of My love that can bathe you and that the living water may flow through you to others."[5]

After God spoke these words, I went to my meeting. I felt elated that day, because I had quality time with the Lord that morning.

GOD WORKS ON MY BEHALF

On January 11, I was 29 weeks along in my pregnancy. My urine test was positive for protein, which again meant that my kidneys were not functioning properly. Contractions began just like the last pregnancy. Fear rose up within me that this baby might arrive early. The Lord spoke to me:

I am going to work on behalf of your health today. Fear not for the child in your womb. This child is mine and I love this child more than you can and will cause no harm to fall upon it. I have a covenant with you. I love you with an everlasting love.

Later that afternoon, I saw my family practice doctor. I realized that God worked for my health. Another passage

---

[5]Catherine Marshall, *Light in My Present Darkness* (Old Tappan, New Jersey: Fleming H. Company, 1986), 180-181.

stood out to me from Catherine Marshall's book, A Closer Walk. At one point in her life, the Lord spoke to her saying:

"A true child of mine has no need to worry, but you act as if you think you have to do everything yourself, as if I, your Burden Bearer, am not with you at all...Each time you experience a negative attitude building up inside yourself, refuse to accept it. Recognize the satanic source of it, reject it, and turn to Me."[6]

That evening, I wrote, "My surprise today was a pleasant conversation with a woman at the clinic's waiting room." I switched from my primary doctor to an OB-GYN specialist. I went there and was greeted warmly by the staff. I felt better knowing that my pregnancy was followed by a specialist.

---

[6]Ibid.,197.

INNER BATTLE RAGES

Krista was fifteen months old in February 1990. Her low weight and poor eating concerned me. She caught the flu and lost more weight. On February 13, we took her to a specialist who ran some tests including one for cystic fibrosis. Mike was especially worried when he read about cystic fibrosis in my pediatric nursing book. Apparently back in 1975, most children with cystic fibrosis only lived until they were 15 years old. I was numb with fear and anxiety.

Krista's upcoming eye surgery for correcting her crossed eyes was scheduled for February 16. The night before, we prayed for her since she still had the flu, and we believed that God wanted us to go ahead with her eye surgery.

The next day, we bundled her up and took her to the surgery center. The surgery was successful, and eventually all her tests came back normal. She did not have cystic fibrosis. We were relieved and grateful.

On Sunday, February 18, I was six and a half months along in my pregnancy, just where I was when Krista was born. My most recent test showed that I did have abnormally high amounts of protein in my urine, which increased my doubts. Could this be a repeat of preeclampsia?

About this time, I had lower abdominal pain on my right side. My doctor thought that the pain was caused by a hernia from my past C-section. He thought that if he did another C-section delivery for this baby, he could repair the hernia at the same time. That was NOT what I wanted to hear, and I didn't want another operation.

Reading scripture and Catherine Marshall's book, I found encouragement. The Lord said:

Be still and I will fight your battle.

THE BATTLE INSIDE CONTINUED TO RAGE

I wrote in my journal, "My life is to be dependent God. I cannot live from crisis to crisis, but must take all to Jesus, every struggle, without the attitude of 'Phew! I'm glad that one is over with!'"

Catherine Marshall's book, *Light in My Present Darkness* ministered to me. I read a part in the book where she described the death of her granddaughter. Catherine wrote how she did not understand why this had happened. She confessed sins of presumption and of not trusting Jesus, not valuing His grace enough, and not abiding in kindness. It was then that Catherine's healing came, and God spoke to her:

> *I, your God, am in everything. Amy Catherine is with Me, and while she lived, she ministered to everyone who prayed for her. You alone, Catherine, were too stubborn to see it.* [7]

That was Catherine's turning point out of darkness. She was given instruction to rise each morning at 6:00 a.m. to rejoice in the Lord. She was to praise Him with a grateful heart, pour out her love, and thank Him for everything that had gone wrong in her life. To focus on praise, she turned to the Psalms.

Reading Catherine's story helped me to see the sovereignty of God in all that had gone wrong in my life. It showed me the importance of praising the Lord in the morning.

Before this, I had focused on what was wrong in my life and resented God for bringing tests my way instead of thanking Him. Catherine Marshall's book reminded me of a better way.

---

[7] Ibid.204.

SELF PITY AND DAMAGED THOUGHTS

On March 10, I heard the Lord's voice again after what seemed like months of darkness and despair in my thoughts. He said:

Do not allow the darkness to seep in. It can come in like a flood to overwhelm you. Look to the Light which will dispel the darkness. Seek help and godly counsel to sort out your disturbing thoughts. I will set you free. Have one more session with your counselor, and she will help you to be free of self-pity and faultfinding which you can fall into so easily.

Grow by My grace. Protect your heart from the enemy that would seek to destroy you by despair and hopelessness. I long to lift you up and stabilize your footing so you don't even stumble. I am the Light that shines in the darkness. My light prevails.

This baby is special to Me and has My protection. I created its inmost being. This child is sealed up until the time of delivery. I long to give you joy in caring for this child. It will be easier than you think. My Presence and peace will guide you with every trivial and great decision. I am your God and bring you this precious gift of a child who will be hand tailored to suit your family. I know what your child and husband need and will not leave them as orphans. Call your counselor, and she will assist you in the natural and also in the Spirit realm. Trust Me with this giant step that seems so great, which is to bring a child into your world. Trust Me for the grace to go through the trials. I will never leave you or forsake you, but will always be with you as a shepherd tends with such care for his own sheep.

You are my own and I bought you with a price. I love you, and you are precious to Me. Let neither the enemy nor your heart deceive you into thinking otherwise. I have chosen you with a special mission in mind: to raise these little ones to know Me as Lord and Savior, and to guide and teach them how to live among the evils of this world. Teach them to know Me as their Father and loving God who will never leave or forsake them. I have entrusted you to hold them in your arms. Be patient to see My hand work out all the details that so easily worry you. Learn of My character and nature. The details and plans will fall into place for you. Fear not, because I know the plans I have for you, plans for a future and a hope.

I will not disappoint you, because I am your God and will take care of your needs. Rest in Me and listen to My voice. When darkness veils My face, look to My unfailing grace.

You are in a valley with Me. Yet, your valley will not last forever. I will take you to the mountaintops. You are an overcomer. You have won the victory in this because of Me. Look to My word regarding valleys. You will find keys to set you free in My word.

IN THE VALLEY

Later in March, I saw my OB-GYN specialist about contractions I was experiencing and I was afraid that he would put me on bed rest. How would I do this with a one and a half year old toddler at home?

In the clinic lobby, I continued my study. I read Joel 3:14 which says, "Multitudes, multitudes in the valley of decision. For the day of the Lord is near in the valley of decision... But the Lord will be a refuge for His people, a stronghold for the people of Israel."

I will be a refuge and stronghold for you, Bonnie. I am your strong, high tower. Whenever you are afraid, run to the tower of refuge which is big enough to contain you. All fears will flee and cannot enter there, once you are hidden in Me, safely within that high tower. Enter now. The battle may rage but you are safe within. No storm can wipe you out. I am your covering.

Ezekiel 37:1 says, "The hand of the Lord was upon me, and He brought me out by the Spirit of the Lord and set me in the middle of a valley. It was full of bones."

I set you in the middle of this valley so you can see that I am God of the Valley. I am with you and will not leave you lifeless as dry bones. I will cause your weariness to become vitality and life once again. As I said to the bones, so I will say, "You will come to life!" Then you will know that I am the Lord.

Ezekiel 37:10 reads, "So I prophesied as he commanded me and breath entered them; they came to life and stood up on their feet—a vast army."

I will again cause you to rise up and take your place. I will not leave you to lose this battle among the ranks. I have set you into a battle, but you will rise victorious. Fear not, for I am with you always. If you can learn to praise Me in the valley, therein will you find the victory.

The songs on my mind were, "I go to the Rock of my Salvation," and "He is my Rock, my Sword, and my Shield." Next, I studied the "Battle in the Valley" in 2 Chronicles 20:1-26. The verse that stood out was 2 Chronicles 20:12, "For we have no power to face this vast army that is attacking us. We do not know what to do, but our eyes are upon You." God's response is in 2 Chronicles 20:15, "Do not be afraid or discouraged because of the vast army. For the battle is not yours but God's."

He gave the Israelites a clear battle plan in verse sixteen, "Tomorrow, march down against them. They will be climbing up by the Pass of Ziz, and you will find them at the end of the gorge on the Desert of Jeruel."

He instructed them in verse seventeen, "You will not have to fight this battle. Take up your positions; stand firm and see the deliverance the Lord will give you…"

Next, I read through Ephesians 6:10-18 about putting on the armor of God, just as I need to for a spiritual battle. I read the rest of 2 Chronicles 20, and worshiped God. He reigns in all circumstances, no matter how difficult.

God met me while I studied scripture as I waited in the doctor's office. When I saw the doctor, he said that I did not need to be on bed rest as I had feared. Thank You, Lord.

THE JOURNEY BEGINS

During my prayer time in March, I wrote, "Thank You, Lord, for this baby within. It is hard to believe that there is actually another life growing inside, a new life with only six weeks before birth. Please give me Your direction for carrying this child."

The Lord spoke:

Rest and wait for Me. Like the Israelites through the desert, you are on a journey. Watch their moves as they were led by Me. Do not murmur, or it will set you back. You can be close to Me or far away. I love you and will never leave you. Begin reading and I will quicken truths to you.

I read more from Catherine Marshall's book, *Light in My Darkest Night*, and the Lord spoke to me:

In the Old Testament, the Israelites were guided by the cloud. In the New Testament, and now, it is My Spirit within you who will guide you. Stay within hearing range of My still small voice within you. I will keep you on the path chosen for you. Do not jump ahead with your own plans. I will quicken this word to you in times of testing, which is only to remind you not to murmur or complain. Remain close to Me and learn from the trials.

A grateful and thankful heart is what I long for. Perseverance will produce My character within you. Rely on My grace. Call out to Me. I love you and will not leave or forsake you ever. You are precious to Me. You will come forth as a flower in the desert with a fragrance sweet to my nostrils. When others smell it, and wonder about your relationship with Me, tell them. A rough diamond needs chiseling to bring forth the brilliance of a sparkling jewel.

I AM CHANGING YOU

One day in March, the Lord impressed these words:

Rest in Me. I am working on your character to bring lasting change. When dross rises to the surface, it will be skimmed off. I use these circumstances in your life to make the flaws in your human flesh nature rise to the surface and to identify them as temptations. The temptations will be there the next time, but you will be able to name them. Bring every temptation to Me, including the awful feelings you had last night. Write them down. You are not responsible for changing them. Confess them to Me and be willing to let Me change your responses to a sincerely loving attitude. I am working to cleanse you of these thoughts and turn your wrong responses into right ones that will please My Father.

I read John 15:1-8 about the branch pruned because it had not received sap from the vine. We cannot bear fruit by ourselves. Remain in the Lord to bear lasting fruit which will be to the Father's glory.

HOPE WITHIN A TRIAL

On March 21, Mike and I talked for two hours after Krista went to bed. I was totally devastated when he shared the struggle he had in his thoughts. I didn't say a word. I drove my car to the St. Croix River. Instead of crossing the bridge to Wisconsin, I drove home.

Although what he had said affected me deeply, I was confident that God would bring me through this great trial. My thoughts rehearsed our conversation. I prayed, "This struggle is bigger than I can handle, Lord. I don't know where to go or who to turn to. I feel isolated, yet, who do I share this with? I am weary of handling this on my own."

That night, I had a dream that I forgave someone. In this dream, that person was not Mike, yet I realized that this dream was important. God knew that I needed this dream to reveal my unforgiveness, resentment, and bitterness. My prayer was, "Thank You, Lord. I am full of gratefulness and thanksgiving. Oh, Hallelujah! You gave me new life. Thank You, Lord, for giving me a new start, for lifting the heaviness, and bringing me out of the desert. When I thought that Mike's confession was too much, You gave me hope."

God brought me through. He promised the trial would end, and it did. He said:

> Stand on the Rock. Come to Me and I will give you rest. This conflict will be resolved and its fruit will be evident to all. Learn from it. Soon, the lesson will be clear. Appreciate and value each other. Come to Me.

THE TRIAL CONTINUES

A few days later, I still struggled with my thoughts toward Mike. Something in our relationship needed to change. I asked the Lord to show us what that next step should look like. We could not go on like this with the tension between us. The Lord asked me:

> How much are you willing to lay down to revive your relationship with each other? Rest in Me, and you will see changes.

The next night, I experienced a breakthrough with Mike. I prayed, "Praise You, Lord. You work all things together for good to them that know You and are called together for Your purposes."

ABOUT THE NEW BABY

The due date for this baby was April 26. A few weeks before, these words came to me:

This child is sealed up in your womb and you are doing great. Do not overdo now. Balance your time. Be wise.

Come to Me for counsel. Listen to My still, small voice and for confirmation of My peace. Let Me put your priorities in order. Today is the beginning of something new. Don't spend time on the trivial, and don't fret that you'll miss something important.

Rest in Me. Allow others to do the major cleaning. Krista needs your attention. Keep correspondences short. People will understand. Make up the list for envelopes to address. It will be easier than you think. Use long envelopes. Stamps are all you need for the birth announcements. Everything will fall into place. Look for your address pages and your calendar date book. Send a card to your sister. Prepare the downstairs, too, for company. I will be with you. Rest often. Rest in My love for you and lastly, give all of your worries to Me.

C-SECTION OR NORMAL DELIVERY

Earlier in this pregnancy, I had developed an incisional hernia from my past C-section delivery of Krista. My doctor planned to repair it at this C-section delivery scheduled for April 23, only nine days away.

At music ministry practice, others prayed for me. One lady believed that my hernia would heal and I would not need a C-section.

Later, I asked the Lord about this. He replied:

You do not have all the facts yet for this delivery, and it is not a time to prepare for something you know little about. Trust the judgment of the expert whom you chose, and trust Me that I will guide him to make the wisest decision for you.

THE DECISION IS MADE

My next doctor's appointment was on April 18. I gladly explained that I didn't have any right-sided abdominal pain from the hernia. He decided to cancel the C-section, and I experienced peace.

After my appointment, I went to a friend's house and she prayed with me. I again felt peace and the Presence of the Lord. I asked Him to help me sort through what others shared and glean only what I would need for this birth.

GIVING ALL FEARS TO GOD

Because I could not shake my fears about childbirth, I needed someone to talk and pray with me. An older friend who was single and had no children came to mind. I called and asked if I could visit. She suggested that before I came, I would write down all my fears. I wrote:

- *Fear of pain and how I might react in labor.*

- *Fear of something happening to me, such as having chest pain or a heart attack because childbirth and labor can be taxing on the heart, and I had not prepared for this marathon experience by exercising. I was not in shape and feared my cardiovascular system might not be able to respond well.*

- *Fear that my kidneys might shut down or I'd experience toxemia.*

- *Fear of losing control of my emotions when the pain became intense.*

- *Fear of being a bad witness to my doctor if I swore or yelled at Mike or the doctor.*

- *Fear of giving up and say, "Just perform a C-section."*

- *Fear of missing Krista because having a C-section required a five-day hospital stay for recovery. Then I couldn't see her during that time.*

- *Fear of my reaction to the newborn baby. I am so close to Krista and feared that might change once the baby was born.*

- *Mainly, though, I feared pain.*

In my friend's apartment, I shared with her my list of fears. We prayed about each one until we felt free to move on to the next.

Her prayers were powerful. My burden of fears lifted. I knew I was free of them, and I could go ahead fearlessly into labor.

Of all the people who helped rid me of fears, it was my friend who never married and had no children who helped the most. Psalm 34:4 says, "I sought the Lord and He heard me, and delivered me from all my fears." He surely did, and I praised and thanked Him for giving me that special friend.

IMPENDING LABOR

Monday, April 23 would have been my C-section, but thank God I didn't go through with it. God's wisdom and plans prevailed. I felt as if my water might have started breaking, but I wasn't sure. I asked Mike to pray for me. At 9:00 a.m. I called the clinic and they wanted me to come in to be checked. Their exam showed I was not yet in labor. Nothing more happened this day, so I rested in bed.

At 12:30 a.m. on Tuesday, April 4, I woke up with mild cramping in my uterus and back. I couldn't sleep, so I called a friend who lived in Hawaii. She was awake because of the time difference, so we talked and prayed for each other. I still had cramps when I hung up the phone, but it wasn't uncomfortable. I stayed up until 5:30 a.m. and used that time to address birth announcement envelopes, read, pray, and finally lay on the couch.

When Mike woke up, I became tired. We prayed, as I was sure that I was experiencing the beginning of labor, but went back to bed. Mike said he would watch Krista and stay home from work.

At 8:00 a.m. my contractions were ten minutes apart. They were different from the Braxton Hicks "false contractions" I had earlier in the sixth month of this pregnancy. These were more like rhythmic menstrual cramps. I called Mom and Dad and asked if they would drive to our house as planned to watch Krista while I went into labor. My aunt came over until my folks arrived. She was a tremendous help, which allowed Mike to leave for work.

In the afternoon, the nurse called and asked how I was doing. When I told her about the contractions, she suggested that I go for a walk to speed things up. As I walked along Greenhaven Drive, Mom and Dad drove by and we rode back to our house together.

By evening, my contractions became stronger. At 12:30 a.m. on Wednesday April 25, we checked into the hospital. I had a wonderful Christian nurse who said she would pray for us.

By 2:30 a.m., I talked to the doctor, and he agreed to give me medication so I could sleep. About 8:30 a.m., another doctor asked if I would rather have a C-section, go home and rest, or stay. When I didn't make progress after an hour, we decided to go home. Although I was disappointed to return without a baby, it was great to see Krista, and she was happy to see me.

I stayed in bed most of the day to get some sleep. Krista, who was upstairs with my mom and dad would call, "Mama? Mama?" When she would crawl downstairs, I lifted her into bed with me. My contractions were not strong, but more frequent at seven to ten minutes apart. By evening, they strengthened. Krista mimicked the "Sss" sound I made while holding my breath with each contraction. At 10:00 p.m., I knew it was time to go back to the hospital.

In the labor and delivery section, I was given a room, but felt uncomfortable with the nurse on duty who didn't smile at all. I secretly called her "Nurse Wretched." When she checked me, I was dilated to three or four centimeters. At least there was some progress.

Although the nurse gave me medication to help ease the pain, still, I could not sleep. However, Mike slept in the chair beside my bed. I knew that my doctor would be on call starting at 7:00 a.m. "Nurse Wretched" would be off duty at 7:30 a.m. Hopefully, I would get a new nurse who would be more pleasant.

BIRTH EXPERIENCE

The morning of April 26 finally came. My doctor was on call and I relaxed. At 8:00 a.m., the new nurse and her co-worker greeted me. She checked, and I was dilated to six centimeters. My water broke then and I experienced hard contractions. I asked Mike to call Mom and Dad and tell them the progress. I felt like I was climbing a high mountain. When I reached the point of transition, the stage of labor when I had heard that some women's emotions go crazy, I threw off the sheets and thrashed about. I was hot and in so much pain with contractions getting close together.

When my cervix was fully dilated to ten centimeters, my doctor was called. I was so glad to see him when he arrived. At that point, I asked for medication to ease the pain. By 10:30 a.m. I could not feel when it was time to push, so the nurse who monitored my contractions told me, according to monitor readings. When the monitor showed a contraction was about to begin, she said, "Here comes another one," so I positioned myself to get ready to push again.

When my doctor said, "That was a good push," I knew I had discovered the right position and targeted that position for each contraction.

I pushed for thirty-five minutes until he said, "I see the baby's head with lots of hair."

By then I was in much pain, but with one more push, the baby's head was born. Then, he said, "Now push once more to get the shoulders out." Ugh! I thought I was done pushing. But with one more push, the baby was out. I felt exhausted as if I had run a marathon.

"Bonnie, you have a little boy," my doctor exclaimed! He was born at 11:07 a.m., on Thursday, April 26, 1990, and weighed eight pounds and four and one-fourth ounces. Mike cut the umbilical cord, which he said was like cutting a thick rubber band. Then he picked up his camera to capture those early moments on film. He also started the tape recorder to record our son's first cries. When I held him in my arms, I saw that his face was terribly bruised, and I felt badly for him. He had probably slid across my tailbone during the hard contractions. He'd had a hard time, too. Finally we were left alone to enjoy our baby. Although I was weak and sore, I was able to nurse him and he did well.

MIRACLES OF BRIAN'S BIRTH

Mike and I named our newborn son Brian Edward Connolly. According to the Urban Dictionary and Wikipedia, the name "Brian" is of Celtic and Irish origin and means "strength, honor, and noble." His middle name "Edward" is an English name that means "Guardian, Protector, Wealthy, and Blessed Guard." Our last name "Connolly" is an Irish surname which means "Faithful to Pledges," and "Not for Himself." If I chose one meaning for Brian's full name, it would be, "Irish and English guardian, protector, wealthy and blessed, full of strength, honor, and nobility, faithful to pledges, and not for himself."

Thank You, Lord, for all the miracles of Brian's birth:

- *He was born when my doctor was able to deliver him. This was a miracle in itself, because the doctor was off duty from Tuesday, April 24, at 5:00 p.m. until Thursday morning April 26 at 7:00 a.m. but entered the labor room just in time.*

- *Upon my arrival at the hospital at 10:00 p.m. on Wednesday evening, April 25, I locked horns with the nurse whose help I did not want during delivery. When she went off duty at 7:30 a.m., a wonderful nurse was assigned to me.*

- *Strong contractions began at 8:00 a.m., and by 10:15 a.m., I was ready to push.*

- *At 11:07 a.m., Brian was born. Other than his badly bruised face, he was a healthy baby.*

God breathed life into this baby, and that was a wonderful miracle.

FIRST DAYS AFTER BRIAN'S BIRTH

The next day, our parents and pastor came to visit. On Saturday, April 28, we were discharged from the hospital.

Krista was excited to see us, and I was grateful to be home. She leaned over the cradle and gently kissed Brian, which was such a precious never-to-be forgotten moment.

That first night at home, Brian slept in a cradle by our bed until midnight, when I changed his diaper and nursed him. He was wide awake until 5:00 a.m. By dawn, I was exhausted, and slept.

Over the next two to three nights, he kept the same routine, woke up at midnight, ate, and stayed awake until 5:00 a.m. After several days, he adjusted and slept later.

In early May, I experienced postpartum depression. When I spent time with God, He reminded me that He is the One who makes and keeps promises. His word says that He would deliver me from everything, even postpartum depression. God is in control. He is the Lord of the Valleys.

On May 6, the robins sang early that morning and in the late afternoon, which reminded me to sing praises and thank God. I read the *Streams in the Desert* devotional book by Mrs. Charles Cowman. The entry for May 5 spoke about how everything comes to us from God's hand. I was thankful for that time to record Brian's first few days in this world. Mike's mom was with us and all was quiet in the house.

Mike's mom stayed for a week in May, and then my aunt stayed from Thursday through Saturday. I was very grateful for their help. I did find it challenging to manage two children, yet with God's help, survived it all.

My first day alone with Krista and Brian was May 14. I practically begged Mike to stay home from work as I was overwhelmed at the thought of taking care of two children alone. I experienced a few trying moments, but by 5:30 p.m., all was quiet with Krista and Brian down for naps.

FAULTFINDING

One of my counselor friends from northern Minnesota stayed with us from May 14 through May 18. We had several important conversations. During her stay, I asked her for personal counsel and she commented on my faultfinding tendencies.

She said, "My first thought even before reading your journal is that faultfinding is a way we use to try to make ourselves appear better in our own eyes and/or in the eyes of the one we are communicating with. As we come to know who we are in Christ, the faultfinding lessens, and eventually becomes a part of our past."

I answered, "Faultfinding is sin."

"Yes it is," she continued, "however, just giving it to the Lord without coming to terms with it, owning it, looking for its source, is like asking God to be a magician."

"Then I give my faultfinding to the Lord."

"Yes, but willingness takes persistence and is an ongoing willful choice to die to something. I believe there are things we can do to solidify our 'death' in the areas needed. One is staying in constant prayer and praise regarding choices we face. A second is immediately confessing our temptation to find fault as soon as the Holy Spirit makes us aware of an episode starting. We may also need to apologize to the other person, perhaps Mike, and change the conversation's direction. Lastly, be quick to speak good, encouraging observations about that person—not just to them, but speak these thoughts aloud to yourself, especially when you feel sorry for yourself. Faultfinding generally precedes or follows self pity, they are twin devils.

"In your journal entry for March 4, you said, 'The Spirit of God was not there.' When we have been unkind to our spouse but then try to commune with God, scripture tells us to first make it right. Remember, loving your neighbor works in proportion to how you love yourself. If you constantly find fault with yourself, Bonnie, you will do that with others as well. For that reason, I sense that tonight may be far more meaningful than either of us may realize. Looking back on the episodes that have been most fruitful, I see that each has had certain elements in common. They have been emotional and come after an outburst of a controlled or uncontrolled emotion. They require patience and perseverance on both parts to be followed with truthful honesty as we see it."

She added, "Our pastor said, 'The most effective way to dishonor another is to not communicate with that person.' To be honest with another can be difficult. When we presume what they will say, how they might react, and what they might think, we dishonor them, thinking the worst and not the best of them. Personally, I want you to believe that I am emotionally and spiritually mature enough to receive your honesty when given in love. That does not mean you are not free to make a mistake in what you say or how you say it, just that love is in it. Also, I pray you trust me, even when you lash out, and it doesn't seem like love is in it. Love is not easily offended."

She spoke further regarding anger and rage. "Bonnie, I just had a thought and wonder if somehow you think, or are programmed to think, that lashing out with anger is effective, while also thinking that anger is unacceptable, and a sin. I wonder if perhaps in your childhood, anger was the emotion that seemed to prove most effective. And yet, as Christians, our instruction is to die to anger. You may also fear that if you tell the truth as you see it, someone will get angry with you, so you do not speak out to confront an issue, hoping it will blow over. Then, if both parties are patient and persevere, it works out to support the belief that you have to lash out to be understood, but at the same time anger brings guilt for the outburst. At any rate, something blocks you from confronting certain issues in honesty, and that makes you beat around the bush. Perhaps anger has been your buddy, and you think it has done you well. Anger has helped you control people and maybe to control conversations. It may not be easy to let go because it has been effective in the past for you. Please know that I am not accusing you—just offering insight for you to consider with an attitude of prayer that God will bring truth."

She shared a story of her own. "When my husband came home late, I would lash out in anger. Finally, God showed me that my underlying emotion was rejection and fear. When I became aware of this, and humbled myself before him, we were able to begin to work it through. In 2 Chronicles 7:14, God says, 'If My people who are called by My name will humble themselves and pray and seek My face and turn from their evil ways, then I will hear them from heaven and will forgive their sin and heal their land.'"

"Humbling ourselves is not just before God but before one another as well. When we let each other know who we are, the good and the bad, we have something to build on. I believe most often people have a struggle with this because of how they feel they have been received, and how they have witnessed others being received, whether they have been honest or humble. I also believe that you have been building a trust in me and especially in Mike, so that you can be free to expose yourself, and that the bouts when you lash out are the times when trusting has been vital but difficult. I suggest we can have the same victory without the anger by humbly revealing where we are and genuinely hearing the others' response in the light of 1 Corinthians 13:4-8. Thank you, Bonnie, for trusting and loving me when I have not deserved your love. Thank you for loving and working with me as God restores me and molds me."

"That makes sense, and you've given me much to think about," I answered.

"Good. I believe you appreciate me and respect me. Sometimes I do not know if you like me, but that is okay. We do not always like our counselors, even though we trust and respect them, because they generally prick our conscience and expose hidden things. That usually hurts and can feel unduly rough. Yet, if God has truly brought the counselor into our path, we need to try to trust even when it hurts. I guess what I say in counseling sessions often makes people feel chastised, and chastisement is not comfortable. In Proverbs 9:8, God says, 'Blessed is the man who wisely receives reproof.' Later in Proverbs 1:23, He adds, 'If you had responded, I would have poured out my heart to you and made my thoughts known to you.' So when I respond to rebuke or reprove or chastise, God will pour His heart out, and make His thoughts known!"

"Today's work was good. It seemed some depth was accomplished without any need for lashing out. I did not sense a forced 'weighing of your words,' but for the most part, free expression of your thoughts and ideas."

I later wrote down her thoughts about expectations: "I believe that the issue of joy is prominent in your thoughts and expectation. Perhaps what you mean by 'expectation' is different from my understanding. Expectation is not altogether a sin. I think not to expect from ourselves, others, and God is not to trust. When we have an 'I deserve...', 'need to...' or, 'ought to...'expectation, then we may move into an unhealthy, unrealistic expectation. For example, when I come to God with a need, I can trust or expect Him to respond. Yet, if I expect him to do it my way or within my time limit, my expectation has moved into an unhealthy, sinful state. Also, good plans established by the sound mind God gave us, and by prayer and meditation, as well as by watchful observation, are not unholy expectations. They are wisdom worked out by our relationship with God and the faith that God through His Holy Spirit will direct our paths."

My friend said, "The joy of the Lord is your strength, Bonnie. When joy comes, you have the strength for whatever task is set before you. God wants you to continue to watch for those things that rob your joy including fatigue, fear of fatigue, self-pity, faultfinding, demands, the 'law' of the word, and unhealthy attitudes. Instead, rejoice in those things that bear the fruit of joy, such as remembering the goodness (and grace) of God to you, the talents He has blessed you with, your family, answered prayers, miracles, friends, spiritual growth, emotional growth, physical health and of course, salvation, and Mike. Read Philippians 4:4-6 which says to 'think on these things', and if we do these things, the Lord will be with us. In the Presence of the Lord, there is joy forevermore. As we transform our thoughts in relationship to Philippians 4:4-9, there is no room for faultfinding or criticism."

"All of this work in our thinking is part of sanctification, and God does what He promises. We may not always like His method, because we often may experience pain, and we've been programmed to believe pain is wrong, and is our enemy. Perhaps we need to rethink the purpose of pain, not to come into sadism, but into balance to accept its purpose and good results."

JOY IN THE LORD

After my friend traveled home on Friday, May 18, I reviewed my time with her.

I am to rejoice and take joy, like taking a cookie in every circumstance, not only in the peaceful, but in chaotic times. The book of Philippians contains the word, "joy" or "rejoice." thirteen times. God will teach me joy as I read through Philippians and learn how to receive joy, practice being joyful, and choose joy in all circumstances. I don't need physical help at this time because I am able to do what God has given me to do. What I am looking for is finding joy in it, finding joy within me and not looking for change in outward circumstances, or having someone make my load easier.

I believe that one of my friend's missions was to remind me of the joy that is within, regardless of my circumstances. As we prayed, the peace of the Lord came and filled me inside. As I read Philippians 1:12-14, the subtitle caught my attention, "Imprisonment a Blessing." Any outward circumstance can be my prison, depending on how I view it. As the passage says, "Rejoice in the Lord always: and again I say, Rejoice" (Philippians 4:4 KJV).

I reviewed scriptures on ways of thinking. "Think on these things." "Renew your mind." I also read the words that another friend said to me recently, "God works to change our thoughts." While we are transforming our thoughts as described in Philippians 4:4-9, there is no room for faultfinding or criticism. Instead it is a sanctification process.

In the past, anger had served me well, but my friend said it can be a way of manipulating. There can be victory without anger by humbly understanding where I am, listening to the other person as 1 Corinthians 13:4-8 states, and enjoying a time of blessing God's name.

"Enjoy this time," she said in her parting words to me. I intend to do just that.

GOD'S PERSPECTIVE ON EMOTIONS

My prayer this June morning was, "Lord, show me a better way to express my feelings when anger, frustration, hurt, rejection, and self pity come my way and invade my thoughts." God's response to me was:

> *All is at rest. Yes, all will be at rest once you come to Me with your reactions to situations that trigger your feelings. I will give you new spiritual eyes to see what happens to you, as I teach you My ways of responding to these things. My rest and peace will be on you to equip you for bringing out what is needed at that time. My timing will be critical, once I have shown you what to do and say. Wait on Me. Don't be quick to lash out and kill with words. Don't be harsh and quick to condemn. Remember, judgment of people and their motives belong to Me. I see what you do not. If you wait on Me, I will give you spiritual eyes to see what I want you to in each situation. It will take practice for you to see this way, and conflicts will arise to give you opportunity to learn. Leaning and waiting on Me quickly will be important.*

Psalm 123:1 came to mind, "I lift up my eyes to you, to you who sit enthroned in heaven."

KEY TO CONTENTMENT

A few days later, when I studied how to train my mind to think according to God's pattern of thinking, He spoke these words to me:

With each situation that arises, I will show you the direction, even which way to think. Here lies the key to contentment. Just as on the path to the mountain village among the rice terraces near Banaue in the Northern Philippines, so I will lead you on the straight and narrow path of the direction for your thoughts. They will become My thoughts, My way of looking at situations or people. Think back on scriptures that have to do with the way of thinking I want you to have.

Passages that came to mind were:

- *Philippians 4:8-9 ~"Whatever is true, whatever is worthy of reverence and is honorable and seemly, whatever is just, whatever is pure, whatever is lovely and lovable, whatever is kind and winsome and gracious, if there is any virtue and excellence, if there is anything worthy of praise, think on and weigh and take account of these things [fix your minds on them]. Practice what you have learned and received and heard and seen in me, and model your way of living on it, and the God of peace (of untroubled, undisturbed well-being) will be with you" (AMP).*

So, I am to think on what is true. I am to tell what is true. Am I tempted to stretch the truth? I am not even to open my mouth and speak that out.

- *Zechariah 8:16 says to speak the truth to one another.*
- *Ephesians 4:25 tells me to speak truthfully to my neighbor.*
- *Psalm 101:7 talks about having no deceit.*
- *Proverbs 12:22 says that the Lord delights in men who are truthful. I am not to have vain imaginations. I am not even to imagine what might be true, only what I know to be true.*

- *2 Corinthians 10:5 ~"We demolish arguments and every pretension that sets itself up against the knowledge of God, and we take captive every thought to make it obedient to Christ."*

Scriptures that talk about "put on" and "put off" refer to a way of thinking.

- *Ephesians 4:22-24 tell me to put off my old unrenewed self and put on a new nature, and to be constantly renewed in the spirit of my mind, having a fresh mental and spiritual attitude, and to put on the new nature (the regenerated self) created in God's image.*

- *Ephesians 6:11-17 refers to me putting on the whole armor of God.*

- *Colossians 3:12-16 talks about clothing myself as God's own picked representative and putting on behavior marked by tenderhearted pity and mercy, kindness, a lowly opinion of one's self, gentle ways, and patience which is tireless and long suffering, and has the power to endure whatever comes, with a good temper.*

These verses exhort me to put on love and let the peace from Christ rule as umpire in my heart (deciding and settling with finality all questions that arise in my mind, in that peaceful state) to which I was called to live (See Colossians 3:15, AMP).

I was challenged to refocus my thoughts on Jesus and not on the problems I may be in the midst of, or that I see around me or within me. I can have two different trains of thoughts:

1. *My problems and situations with people.*
2. *Jesus, the Rose of Sharon, Living Water.*

On August 3, 1984, a prophecy someone gave me referred to thoughts:

"…I shall touch your mind and My mind shall clothe you."

Another prophesy was given to me on September 14, 1984 which spoke about thoughts,

For the former things are passed away. The former things are gone. You need to hear this so that you can step out, even as a tortoise might step out of its shell. You have a need to step out. The Lord would use that example to show even the difficulty of coming out of something that is so natural to you, and it has to do with a way of thinking. The Lord will draw you out and give you a new helmet. Grow not weary or discouraged in your own thoughts to think, "There is no way out for me." But, trust in the Lord, for He works in your thoughts. He works to change your thoughts, and it shall not be by your own willpower. It shall be by the miraculous intervention of your God.

The Lord gave me more insight on His way of thinking:

I wish to change your thoughts. There is a way out for you. I will show you and redirect your thinking, even though the outward circumstances or people around you may never change. Do not count on external things to change. You have been looking at the outward circumstances and people close to you to change and think that if that happened, you would be content, happy and peaceful. That is not so. Let this truth sink into your inner most being. Put your hope and trust in Me alone. Let your roots grow deep in Me. Understand Who I am. Read about and experience Me. I have good things in store for you. They are not external things, but look inwardly to find blessings and good things.

FOCUS ON THE GOOD

The Lord continued to teach me more about His thoughts.

Do not focus on the bad or negative in people or situations. Instead, look for the good.

Two scriptures came to mind: "Cast all your anxiety on him because he cares for you" (1 Peter 5:7 NIV) and "Do not be anxious about anything, but in every situation, by prayer and petition, with thanksgiving, present your requests to God. And the peace of God, which transcends all understanding, will guard your hearts and your minds in Christ Jesus" (Philippians 4:6-7).

These scriptures show a different way of thinking, because I work to change your thoughts. You can choose the direction of your thoughts. Like a train at a switch yard, you have many possible directions in which to think. Be directed to the straight and narrow thoughts of righteousness, purity, truthfulness, honesty, virtue, loveliness, admirable, excellent, praiseworthy, and just.

David's sin with Bathsheba, described in 2 Samuel 11, focused on his train of thought. His eyes saw Bathsheba. He pursued what he saw. David sent someone to find out about her. He acted on what he saw and pursued until he got what he coveted in his heart. She came to him, so she also had a part in this. She could have chosen not to go. Yet, he was the king. She had purified herself from her uncleanness, and she conceived from this single union. However, the baby died, because the union displeased the Lord.

In 1 John 2:16, John describes the lust of the eyes (thoughts), the cravings of sinful man (thoughts again), boasting of what he has in this world (words), and boasting regarding what he does (words).

David was tempted to sin as a result of the lust of his eyes. He could have turned away but got enticed by a craving for a sexual experience. A change of his thoughts could have changed his behavior. He needed to realize that what he might do with Bathsheba would displease God, besides thinking of what harm it would cause to Uriah, her husband, who was in battle, fighting for Jerusalem. David could have thought, "I am already married, and this will greatly damage my relationship with my wife." In any case, he did not heed any warning. His thoughts of sin preceded and empowered his act of sin.

STUDY IN JOSHUA

By the time I settled Brian down to sleep, it was 5:00 a.m. I considered staying up to seek the Lord. My prayer instruction seemed to be, yes, and the Lord impressed these words on me:

Read Joshua 1. This is a new journey, with new territory to be gained, and a new way of thinking. I will give back what the canker worm has eaten away.

The Lord spoke to Joshua, just like He speaks to me. I am to keep in touch with Him. I had a sense of the Presence of the Lord all day long, and hardly ever lost it. I was excited to start on this journey of God teaching me through the book of Joshua about how He would work to change my thoughts. My new way of thinking is my new territory to be gained, just as Joshua gained the literal Promised Land of Israel.

I read the book of Joshua and studied the life of Joshua. He was Moses' aide and may have been discipled by Moses. Deuteronomy 34:9 says, "Now, Joshua, son of Nun was filled with the spirit of wisdom, because Moses had laid his hands on him. So the Israelites listened to him and did what the Lord had commanded Moses."

Then, God spoke to me and I believe He said that He had a plan for me:

You will be a leader of people who will be set free of those emotions that bind them.

Joshua 1:8 says, "Do not let this Book of Law depart from your mouth; meditate on it day and night, so that you may be careful to do everything written in it. Then you will be prosperous and successful." The Lord said,

This is the plan I have for you. I will instruct you in the morning from the book of Joshua, and in the evening, meditate on instructions and words I give you. The daily key to success is to do everything I tell you.

My early thoughts turned to the Lord. He had commanded, and I would obey.

Be of a sound and balanced mind. Do not be led by discouraging negative emotions. Be courageous. I will be with you. Trust Me in every emotional storm. This territory of raising two children is new for you, but I will give you wisdom and direction. I will give you health in body, soul, and soundness of mind to weather the storms of life.

Joshua 1:13 says, "Remember the command that Moses the servant of the Lord gave you: 'The Lord your God is giving you rest and has granted you this land.'" He is also giving me rest from concentrating on this so hard. There is a process of rest, a state of continuous rest.

My direction for helping others comes from Joshua 1:14-15, "You are to help them until the Lord gives them rest, as he has done for you, and until they too have taken possession of the land the Lord your God is giving them. After that, you may go back and occupy your own land, which Moses the servant of the Lord gave you east of the Jordan toward the sunrise."

GO! LOOK OVER THE LAND

On June 21, I worked on my study in Joshua, relating it to emotions and a strong mind, which was my "promised land" at a time in my life when I felt as if my emotions were unstable. Joshua 2:1 says, "Then Joshua son of Nun secretly sent two spies from Shittim. 'Go, look over the land,' he said, 'especially Jericho.'" So they went and entered the house of a prostitute named Rahab and stayed there.

Rahab hid the spies. Later, they returned to Joshua and said, "The Lord has surely given the whole land into our hands; all the people are melting in fear because of us" (Joshua 2:24). Some days later, when the Israelites were going to cross the Jordan, Joshua said to the people, "Consecrate yourselves, for tomorrow the Lord will do amazing things among you" (Joshua 3:5).

I prayed, "Lord, what about tomorrow at church? Please do amazing things in our fellowship at church. We all need a breakthrough!"

Joshua 3:10-17 describes how God was to drive out Israel's enemies. Then when the priests who carried the ark reached the Jordan, and their feet touched the water's edge, the water from upstream stopped flowing, and the people crossed over opposite Jericho. All Israel passed over until the whole nation had crossed on dry ground.

I saw a parallel between the Israelites who began the journey to enter the Promised Land, and my promised land, soundness of mind and balanced emotions. God's Presence in Israel's early days was the Ark of the Covenant, which went before all of Israel. God's Presence will go before me to prepare the way for me to have my promised land and victory to include a sound mind and a mindset of stability in emotions so I can function well.

CROSS THE JORDAN

My study of Joshua continued and I related it to my "promised land" of balanced emotions. I read through Joshua 3:14-17, and contemplated how the Israelites' crossing over the Jordan River paralleled my entry into the new Land of Canaan, the promised land. The areas I wanted to conquer in my life were: fears, worries, angry outbursts, crying with self pity, blaming others for my actions, being ashamed of who I am, and having false guilt.

The Lord goes before us to show the way we have never been before. The Lord by His Spirit responded:

Make one step in the right direction. Do not lose sight of the Ark of the Covenant. Do not even look or focus on the Promised Land. You will reach the other side of the Jordan and set foot on the banks of the Promised Land. Yet, do not focus on that, or even on the battles and victories to be won there. Focus not on the giants in the land. They will be driven out. The battle is Mine. Victory is yours. I will teach you how to war as in Psalm 18. I will show you how to wear and use your armor. Yet, now is the time to look only at My Ark of the Covenant. Turn your eyes upon Jesus. I will show you the rest.

PART THE FLOODWATERS

A few days later, my emotions were still in turmoil, yet the Lord drew me to focus on Him. I read Joshua three and four. The Jordan River was at flood stage at that time of year, but the Lord caused the water from upstream to stop flowing as soon as the priests who carried the ark of the covenant of the Lord set foot in the river. Instead, the water piled up in a great heap a great distance away. After the floodwaters parted, the whole nation of Israel crossed on dry ground.

"Lord, what does this mean for me now?"

He replied:

I parted the waters for the Israelites so they could cross over the Jordan to the other side. There is a way through the waters, even at flood stage, by My mighty hand. When I part the water for you, to make a way for you and Mike in your relationship to get to the other side, work through each conflict, without avoiding or backing away from it. Face it and take one step into the water, and then I will be there to part them. After I do this, write down how I parted the waters as a reminder of how My mighty hand saves you from separa-

tion or divorce. Even if these things would never happen outwardly, you have a tendency to separate and divorce yourself from Mike in your mind. You tend to shut him off and not let him in. Let him in to work out conflicts together.

You use anger to repel him because you know he would not want to come near you when you are angry. It is just like the roaring lion that no one wants to come near, or a prickly porcupine that someone likened you to.

I was puzzled. "Why don't I want Mike near me? Why do I cut him off and not allow him near? Is it manipulation?

The Lord replied:

It is denying him of meeting his needs, because in your eyes, he is not meeting your needs.

My prayer then was, "Lord, help me see the truth through all the floodwaters. Part the waters, Lord. Please give me Your vision. Mike will leave soon on his three day trip, and we have hardly spoken to one another. Please make a way, Lord. Give me the grace to reach out and not roar like a lion. Help us to work things out before Mike leaves."

THINK ON THE POSITIVE

Last night was a time of interrupted sleep with two young children, yet the Lord gave me a new way of thinking about my situation. I prayed, "Thank You Lord for the sleep I did get last night. I slept from 11:00 p.m. to 12:30 a.m., and again from 12:30 a.m. to 4:00 a.m. The Lord spoke to me:

Think on the positive. Be thankful for the good in all circumstances. You are changing. You are becoming less frustrated and angry over incidents. Your children did not willfully keep you from sleep. Don't blame them. They don't know any different. Just let it go. The night is over. Find the

Streams in the Desert passage about the robins. Share that on Wednesday for the Bible Study.

I turned to the reading for May 5 in *Streams in the Desert.*[8] These are God's blessings. He continued:

Call your friend later this morning. Share this with her. Bless her with what I have blessed you. This is the pathway of life. This is the straight and narrow, to look at the situation and see the good in it. Think on these things, as My word says in Philippians 4:8. Do not think on the negative. Sing and praise as freely as the robins outside first thing in the morning and last thing at night.

OLD WAYS OR NEW WAYS

I read Joshua 5:11-12, "The day after the Passover, that very day, they ate some of the produce of the land: unleavened bread and roasted grain. The manna stopped the day after they ate this food from the land. There was no longer any manna for the Israelites, but that year, they ate of the produce of Canaan."

I thought of how the old way of eating manna was practiced until the new way began. When I put on the new, then the old falls apart because it is no longer needed. The Lord gave me a parallel of this principle to my emotional reaction to situations:

Think about this passage in connection with your emotions. The old way of reacting falls away when you see the new way in operation and see the fruit of it in your life. This is the new way of responding, instead of with anger. Let this sink in.

FAITH BECOMES SIGHT

[8] Mrs. Charles Cowman, *Streams in the Desert*, 3d ed. (Grand Rapids, Michigan: Zondervan Publishing House, 1965), 148-149.

I meditated on a passage from Basilea Schlink's book, *Realities*. "When God gives a promise, and you see it in faith, then He will bring it literally into sight in His time."[9] The example used in Basilea's book was how she could visualize a cow in the newly built stall. I remembered visiting a friend in 1985, and while babysitting her foster children I had a vision of me nursing a baby boy. Now, five years later, that vision has become true.

Next, I read in Joshua 6 about the walls of Jericho that fell. I asked the Lord if He would tear down the walls separating Mike and me as He did the walls around Jericho. God told the Israelites that He delivered Jericho into their hands along with its kings and its fighting men before it ever happened. He instructed them to march around the city seven times while the priests blew the trumpets. Then when the people shouted loudly, the wall of the city would collapse and the people could enter straight into the city.

In Joshua 6:6, the Israelites recaptured the Ark of the Covenant of the Lord, and set seven priests the Lord prepared to go before the Israelites sounding trumpets. They marched around the city with the armed guard ahead of the Ark of the Lord. They did not give a war cry until the Lord told them to shout. Then, when the time was right, the Lord said, "Shout, for I have given you the city!" and the walls of Jericho came down.

For today, Jericho represents my marriage relationship with Mike. The walls and barriers between us are like the walls around Jericho. They need to crumble. The Lord said to me:

> *Save what is good from your relationship with Mike. Look for the gold, silver, bronze, and iron articles in it, but burn the rest.*

9M. Basilea Schlink, Realities of Faith, 3d ed. (Phoenix, Arizona: Evangelical Sister of Mary, 1995), 95.

I understood what the Lord meant by this. What is worth saving in our marriage? What are the gold, silver, bronze and iron articles in our marriage? I asked the Lord to show me.

BATTLE PLAN FOR MARRIAGE

One morning, I focused on Joshua 6 and how the wall of Jericho fell, trying to see how the ancient battle applied to God's strategy for our marriage relationship. The Lord said:

You are at the point of the battle for Jericho where the walls are high, just as the walls between you and Mike are high. Here is the key to break down those "Jericho walls" in your marriage. The plan of battle will fool you. It is not by violent means, but by cherishing the treasure in each other and applying the royal law of love. Do these things. Live them out, and then when the walls tumble down, SHOUT, because I have given you the victory. Both of you are to be devoted to Me. Practice the vows you made to one another every day.

If you do this, yours will be a marriage and family known to the world as ones who love each other and walk in My ways.

Mike and I struggled with communication during conflicts. Yet, we were committed to each other and to our marriage. I read Joshua 6 again and looked for clues to breaking down the walls around Jericho.

Look at the words to the song, "SHOUT! For I Have Given You the City." The city represents your marriage. Victory is here even if you haven't experienced it yet. The Israelites shouted before they took the city and before they experienced victory, because The Lord commanded that they shout. You are to do the same. Shout "Victory" in your heart because the Lord has given you victory in communication during conflict in your marriage. Live that way today. Act

139

that way. The enemy inside the walls has come to kill and destroy your marriage, but God has given you victory over Satan and is helping you safeguard your marriage—even though you may not experience it yet. You have authority over Satan in your marriage because God has ordained marriage. It is a covenant not to be broken between God, Mike, and you. Because of this covenant, your marriage will stand against Satan.

- Sound the trumpet. Shout (Joshua 6:20).

    Play victory and battle songs on the piano ahead of time toward victory. God has won it for you and is helping you to have the victory in your marriage. Keep this in mind.

- The wall collapsed (Joshua 6:20).

    Look at the power that was shown by shouting the victory over the walls of the enemy. Remember the song, "Joshua fought the Battle of Jericho, and the walls came tumbling down?" When you sing this song, remember that you have power and authority over Satan in all areas, including your marriage, by the blood of Jesus Christ.

- Charge straight in and take the city (Joshua 6:20).

    Take the bull by the horns. The enemies are the ones to destroy. Think of the Bible teacher who taught on the topic, "Enemies of the Home." He included some things that destroy a marriage and a home.

- Devote the city to the Lord (Joshua 6:21).

    Devote your marriage to the Lord. Marriage is to be upheld in the honor of the Lord, with Him honored as Lord over your marriage.

- Bring out Rehab (Joshua 6:23).

    Rehab had faith in God and she helped the Israelite spies. Therefore, Rehab was placed in the lineage of Christ. He who is not against Jesus is for Him. This is the standard for every friendship. Keep away from those who are against Jesus.

- Destroy every living thing in it (Joshua 6:21, Deuteronomy 20:16-18).

In your home, destroy all things that set themselves up against the knowledge of God. Set the standard high in your marriage and in your home. Don't allow anything to cause you to stumble in these areas. Even sort through your books, tapes, and get rid of the clutter.

- Burn the city. Destroy it completely (Joshua 6:24).

Get rid of all impure things completely. Clean up your behavior. Get rid of anything that sets itself up as rebellion against your marriage. Having independence from Mike and rebellion against his authority are examples. Guard your time, money, relationships, and marriage. Destroy all that is not for your marriage.

- Put articles of gold, bronze, silver, and iron into the treasury of the Lord (Joshua 6:24).

The silver, gold, bronze and iron are precious metals for God's treasury to be kept to beautify the tabernacle and its services. The tabernacle is a house for the Lord, for servant-hood to others, especially for the household of faith. Dale Garrett's book, "The Pleasure of Your Company" may help you better understand how you can make your home welcoming for company.[10]

- Don't rebuild the city again (Joshua 6:26).

Don't go around the mountain again. Learn from your mistakes, especially concerning rebellion or submission to Mike in the areas of finances, time management, and household cleanliness. Don't fight about it.

---

10 Dale Garrett, The Pleasure of Your Company 2d ed. (Eastbourne, E. Sussex, England: Kingsway Publications, 1984).

- Remember, God is with you, as He was with Joshua (Joshua 6:27).

Never forget about My ever present help in time of need. I am not some kind of mouse in a corner. I am the Living God, the Creator of the universe, the Creator of marriage as a covenant before Me. I am present now. I am with you and Mike now.

- Fame will spread through the land (Joshua 6:27).

Yours will be a marriage and family known to the world as ones who love each other and walk in My ways. Go in My name proclaiming that Jesus reigns. Now is the time for the church to proclaim Jesus as Savior, Redeemer, and Lord!

VICTORY OVER ANGER

In July, I read Joshua 8. These words from the Lord showed the parallels between my anger and the Israelite's Battle at Ai.

I gave the Israelites victory over Ai as I will with your anger. Don't think it is hopeless. I know the roots and triggers of your anger. Let Me show you a better way to express anger. It will be different with each case, yet the principles, based on love, remain the same. Look over the notes that you found on anger and strife. There you will find the keys.

Several scriptures that stood out to me in my study:

- *Proverbs 19:11 – "A man's wisdom gives him patience; it is to his glory to overlook an offense."*

- *Proverbs 21:9 – "Better to live on a corner of the roof than share a house with a quarrelsome wife."*

- *Proverbs 21:19 – "Better to live in a desert than with a quarrelsome and ill-tempered wife."*

- *Proverbs 21:23 – "He who guards his mouth and his tongue keeps himself from calamity."*

- *Proverbs 16:32 – "Better a patient man than a warrior, a man who controls his temper than one who takes a city."*

- *Ecclesiastes 7:9 – "Do not be quickly provoked in your spirit, for anger resides in the lap of fools."*

- *James 1:19 – "My dear brothers, take note of this: Everyone should be quick to listen, slow to speak, and slow to become angry, for man's anger does not bring about the righteous life that God desires."*

- *Proverbs 17:14 – "Starting a quarrel is like breeching a dam; so drop the matter before dispute breaks out."*

- *Proverbs 20-3 – "It is to a man's honor to avoid strife, but every fool is quick to quarrel."*

I gladly kept in mind that God said He would give me the victory over anger.

A LIFE OF LOVE

I meditated on James 1:19-22 and personalized these verses to read, "Bonnie, take note of this: be quick to listen to Mike, slow to speak, and slow to become angry with him, for your anger does not bring about the righteous life that God desires. Therefore, get rid of all the moral filth and evil that is so prevalent and humbly accept the word planted in you, which can save you. Don't just listen to the word and so deceive yourselves. Also do what it says, and keep a tight rein on your tongue."

I am to "live a life of love." This is my watchword for the coming year beginning on August 18, 1990. Last year it was, "The Year of Reconciliation."

God has given me a new "watchword" each year since I was in the Philippines on August 18, 1987.

REASONS FOR MY ANGER

When I say my emotions are up and down, I realized that I am "down" when a conflict or problem is not resolved. When it is resolved, I am "up" again, so I pondered the reasons why I feel anger.

I become angry when our children are demanding, or when more demands are placed on me than I think I can handle. I know I should meet our children's needs joyfully, and feel guilty when I express anger.

I feel frustrated when I don't get the sleep I need. I feel tired when my sleep is frequently interrupted. If I feel rested, I don't mind waking up at night to care for our children.

I become upset when I feel misunderstood, unloved, or unappreciated. And then I feel guilty about being self-centered if I express those feelings.

When conversations are too superficial, if I don't share my struggles, or if no one else shares their struggles on a heart to heart level, I become frustrated.

My prayer was, "Lord, help me know where to go from here."

MIRACLE TRIP TO MONTANA

During a conversation that I had with my cousin on April 23, I mentioned that a major speaker in YWAM and a worship leader from the Hawaii YWAM base were scheduled to speak and lead worship at a "Vacation with a Mission" (VWAM) week at the YWAM base in Lakeside Montana. I asked her to consider joining our family as a nanny on this trip.

Shortly after our conversation, she applied to be a nursery worker for the VWAM in July. The staff in Montana accepted her application, and I was elated! We sent in our registration for the VWAM as well. Now, nearly three months later, we prepared for our trip.

Who would have guessed that a trip like this would take place? My cousin was our nanny for Krista, who was twenty months old, and for Brian who was two months old, and for the other children in the nursery as well.

Other major events happened in July. I developed three infections requiring two rounds of antibiotics. Mom suffered her fifth heart attack, and was transported to Fargo, North Dakota, to wait for quadruple coronary bypass surgery, scheduled for July 4. Mike and I struggled with the decision of whether we should drive to Fargo to be with Mom, if both of us should stay home, or if I should drive to Fargo alone, as Mike couldn't get time off from his job. After much prayer, we believe God showed us that we were to stay together at home, so I could recuperate from my infections. We decided to see Mom and Dad on our way to Montana.

Mom miraculously recovered from her surgery, while Krista, Brian, and I caught colds, our car leaked oil, and only two days remained before we should leave on our trip. What more could go wrong? In prayer, the Lord said to me:

> *No, the question is, what more could go right? I am on the throne. This trip is to be bathed in prayer, morning, and evening, and everything sandwiched in between. You will see miracles happen with wonderful answers to prayer. Keep mental notes. Ponder them in your heart. You will draw close to me as never before, and see My miraculous hand and power deliver you from all difficulties. Trust Me to see you through, and let not a day go by that you don't praise and thank Me for all that I have done. I work for your good, and the plans that I have for you are mighty. You will see strongholds torn down and even sense freedom in the air.*

> *Bathe in My love and love for one another. Read through Proverbs daily, corresponding to the date. Remember, we are still working through your anger, using Joshua's battle at Ai in Chapter 8. This will be your battle plan to give you keys for victory. Proverbs will also give you watch words to control your tongue in times of heated battles.*

I turned to Proverbs 15, since it was July 15, and found the following keys:

- *Gentle answers only. No harsh words to stir up anger. Repel harshness by gentleness.*

- *Watch your words when you are angry.*

- *Let your tongue bring healing, instead of crushing another's spirit.*

- *Be discerning. Be on your guard when you sense trouble. Don't give way to anger. Guard your tongue.*

- *Be patient. Calm a quarrel. Don't stir up dissension. Don't be hot tempered.*

- *Be humble. This comes before honor.*

CHILDREN ARE A BLESSING FROM GOD

One day in July as I prayed, the Lord spoke to me about Brian:

Brian is part of the healing of Krista's birth experience. Look at how I could have taken her Home then, but didn't. I chose to give you great joy in seeing her at this age, which you would have missed, had she died then. Trials will always come and go, yet amidst the trials are blessings like enjoying Krista as she is today. Blessings come to give you joy.

Brian's was also a miracle birth. I could have chosen to take him Home at any time during your pregnancy. If I had, you would have missed his smiles and laughter.

Your level of faith has grown from Krista's birth to Brian's. Share with others how I healed you and your children. Give testimony to Me when you do; you are giving Me the glory. Look back and be reminded of Krista and Brian's birth and you will learn more of My character and nature by doing so. I am a good Father and love you as My child. I desire to give you good and perfect gifts, like Brian and Krista to enjoy. They are some of my greatest blessings to you.

KEYS FROM PROVERBS ON THE TONGUE

On Tuesday, July 17, we were to leave for Montana. In the morning I went through Proverbs 17 to look for more keys to control my tongue:

- *Better to have very little, just even a dry crust of bread, than feast with strife. I bought too many groceries yesterday that were wants, not needs. In the future, I was to be content to stay on the grocery list and be on a budget.*

- *My children are a crown to my mom and dad. Let Mom and Dad enjoy them.*

- *Don't start a quarrel. Drop it, and hold your tongue.*

As our trip to Montana began, we stopped to see Mom and Dad in Akeley, Minnesota. Mom looked terribly weak and pale from her surgery. Yet, both of them enjoyed Krista and Brian immensely. I am so grateful that Mom pulled through the surgery, and I am so glad that they were able to get help from a public health nurse and a home agency.

After visiting Mom and Dad, we began our trek to Montana, but took our time and stopped often.

On Saturday July 21, we arrived in Apgar Village in Glacier National Park, Montana. That morning, the Lord spoke to me:

> *Don't let a day go by without praising and thanking Me. Don't rush. The details of the trip will fall into place. I'm on the throne and have your best interest in mind. You will know My will by the peace in your heart. Hold on to the good, but don't hold onto grudges. Instead, give them to Me.*

REFRESHMENT INSTEAD OF FATIGUE

At the "Vacation With A Mission" (VWAM), I prayed, "Lord, things must get easier. Change my way of thinking toward this life with two small children. I am exhausted and need refreshment."

On the first day, there was a time of worship, and people began to dance as they praised the Lord. God said:

> *The time of dancing was for your benefit, to let you know that I am counteracting your fatigue, tiredness, and exhaustion in your physical body.*

Thank You, Lord! I felt refreshed and ready to take on the tasks in front of me. God is so good to give us what we need, if we only ask.

KRISTA'S MIRACLE HEALING

On July 27, Krista's fever was 104.2. I couldn't believe it could be so high. I felt panic so I took it again and found it to be 103. We were supposed to leave the YWAM base the following day to head home.

That next day, I asked some people we knew to pray for Krista. As we drove off, she still looked pale and listless as she slept in the van.

The following day we put her back in the van to drive the next leg of the journey. She looked so still while she slept that it scared me. We prayed once again and asked God to touch her. As we looked up, we saw a double rainbow and took this as a promise that God intends to heal her.

When Krista woke up sweating, I sighed with relief, knowing that her fever had broken! At our friends' home, I checked her temperature and found it had dropped to 101. Her fever the next day was normal. Praise God! She drank a lot of juice and went back to sleep.

"Thank You, God for healing Krista." This definitely was a miracle.

At the next motel where we stayed, the electricity went out. By flashlight, while everyone else was asleep, these words came to me:

I am working in this too. Don't forget about Me. Remember that I have a perfect time for you to leave on Wednesday. My purposes prevail. Leave everything in My hands. Submit to what Mike says about leaving. Don't manipulate anything to bring about what you want, which may be triggered by false guilt or expectations. Don't be guided by others' plans to fit their wants and desires. Leave things alone. It will work out."

Everything did work out. Mike was able to get an extension on his vacation, and did not need to return to work until Thursday. Praise the Lord!

WARS AGAINST US

The eighth chapter of Joshua describes how the city of Ai was destroyed. I likened Ai to my anger when it becomes sin. Sometimes I scream and control others with my angry outbursts, in an attempt to have my own way. This use of my angry outburst is inappropriate. God told Joshua not to be discouraged or afraid. He instructed him to attack according to God's strategy. They were to surround the city of Ai, move in on it, then kill the enemy. They were to build an altar to the Lord and worship God. Joshua was to read the law that Moses commanded, so everyone had an opportunity to hear the word of the Lord.

In Joshua nine, kings and leaders of the enemy met together and made war against Joshua and Israel. That is what I experienced yesterday when everyone seemed to demand my attention. I felt as if everything closed in on me, inside and out. Today was a better day.

My inappropriate, angry response caused me to yell, scream, throw something, slam a door, storm off somewhere, quit or change jobs, change churches, change boyfriends while I was single, not write a letter to a friend, or not call a friend if I carried an offense. Anger handled this way never works. Instead, the problem is ignored or fought in a wrong way. God wants me to come to Him for strength and grace to endure the pressures and gain wisdom to see through Satan's trickery. Instead, I can receive God's strategy for necessary confrontations and receive the power to war against them. In Joshua's time, all the enemies came together to make war against Joshua and Israel because they had not inquired of the Lord.

When Joshua marched from Gilgal to Makkedah, the Lord said to Joshua, "Do not be afraid of them; I have given them into your hand. Not one of them will be able to withstand you" (Joshua 10:8).

Joshua took the enemy by surprise. The Lord threw them into confusion before Israel, who defeated them in a great victory at Gibeon. The Lord hurled large hailstones down on them from the sky, and more of them died from the hailstones than were killed by the swords of the Israelites.

On the day the Lord gave the Amorites over to Israel, Joshua spoke to the Lord, and said in the sight of Israel, "O sun, stand still at Gibeon, O moon, over the Valley of Ajalon!" So the sun stood still, and the moon stopped, till the nation avenged itself on its enemies, as is written in the Book of Jashar" (Joshua 10:12-13). Scripture tells us the sun stood still in the middle of the sky and delayed going down about a full day, and the moon stayed until Israel took vengeance upon their enemies. There was no day like it before or since, when the Lord heeded the voice of a man, for the Lord fought for Israel. Similarly, He will fight for me. He will rout the enemy for me, because He knows my hurting heart desires to win the battle and control my anger. The Lord said:

> You've fought. You've prayed. You've tried in your own strength to control your anger, all without avail. Now is the time to lay down your own weapons of defense, and let Me throw the enemy into confusion. Let Me fight this battle before you.
>
> Come to Me in the heat of the battle, or better, when you see the battle approaching, for the plan and the strategy. Each battle plan is different. I may throw the enemy into confusion, or pour down hail from heaven and destroy them all.

Come to Me and don't speak until you do. Even your unspoken words and thoughts can do mighty damage. Unload it all on Me. Put on My thoughts and words like a mantle, whether I choose to have you speak or be silent. Remember, I caused the enemy to be confused. I sent great hail to fall and killed more of them than by the sword. I made the sun to stay still for a full day while the battle raged. There will be supernatural aid to win battles. Then, praise Me for the victory.

RECONCILIATION WITH MIKE

On August 18, God gave me a new watchword for the coming year, "This is a year for reconciliation with Mike." He spoke these words:

Breaking down barriers in communication will happen. Intimacy like you have never dreamed possible will happen, even with romance. Conflicts will resolve quickly. You have a strong foundation in your relationship. Now is the time to knock down crumbling walls and start over to learn new ways to cope and communicate. You have two lovely children. You and Mike are a good match.

This morning, I read Joshua 11:5, "All these kings joined forces and made camp together at the Waters of Merom, to fight against Israel." Sometimes I sense the forces of evil gang up to fight against me. In the next verse, the Lord encouraged Joshua by saying not to be afraid of the enemies. He told Joshua that He would hand his enemies over to Israel to be slain.

God persuaded me not to be afraid of unseen enemies, because He would slay them. He will help me overcome hidden enemies such as discouragement, fear, and worry.

CARES AND BURDENS OF THE LORD

A friend called early one morning. I was sobered as she unloaded her burden onto me. I asked the Lord if it was right to carry her burden, or if I was carrying a burden that

He did not mean for me to carry. Years ago, I had received a prophecy about bearing burdens:

…There are those who would become a burden and wear you down with their problems when they don't mean to do anything about them. The Lord shall give you wisdom to understand, and you shall give that which the Lord gives and shall cut it off, not with the wrong spirit, but because of what the Spirit of the Lord says regarding it. You shall distinguish between the cares that are truly yours and the cares of another that would make you carry, which are not a burden of the Lord has for you.

…Cast your care upon Me as My word declares, and surely the burden of the Lord shall not weary you, nor exhaust you, nor make you weary, but with joy and with lightness you shall bear it. And when you have borne it, and in your faithfulness have completed that which I have put on you, I shall lift it. Don't try to put it on again and walk under the mantle of it. I shall be the one that shall minister abundant life.

Then, I asked the Lord about my friend who called. I was so burdened by what she had shared:

As for your friend, she is one who sometimes burdens you with her problems but doesn't mean to do anything about them. She is not tackling her problems in My way with the humility and obedience that I desire. Wait on Me, and I will give you the prayer direction for her, as she requested you to pray for her.

Give what I give and cut it off, not with the wrong spirit, but because of what the Spirit of the Lord says regarding it. Don't carry the weight of her burden any longer. It is not meant for you to carry. These are the cares of another that are not a burden from Me. Cast your care on me. The burden of the Lord is not meant to weary you, nor exhaust you.

I responded, "Thank You, Lord. I cast my care upon You. Her burden did weary me, so it was not a burden I was to carry. Thank You for carrying her burden, and thank You for showing me the difference."

PLANS FOR THE DAY

During a time with God, I reviewed His plan for the Israelites on their way to the Promised Land. First, they entered the land. Next, they conquered and divided the land, which took seven full years of battle. Suddenly, it seemed as if the Lord interrupted my reading and said,

> *I do not want you to go shopping today. I would like you to be in prayer for your friend, and for your mom, like the Levites did. They offered up sacrifices and prayers to Me on the Israelites' behalf. You already have a suitable outfit for Saturday night, so you don't need to go shopping for another one.*

That settled my plan for the day, and I stayed home. Instead, I continued reading in Joshua fourteen, and did what the Lord asked me to do.

MAKING MISTAKES

At 8:00 a.m. on Monday, August 20, a team from Youth With A Mission that stayed at our house was ready to leave. I overslept and felt guilty. They were supposed to leave by 7:30 a.m.

At 7:00 a.m., I felt as if Jesus wanted to spend time with me, but I was too tired and went back to bed. I thought of Psalm 145:14, "The Lord upholds all those who fall and lifts up all who are bowed down." Proverbs 24:16 reads, "...for though a righteous man falls seven times, he rises again..." God responded to my cry:

> *I am testing you, and though you may fail the test in your own eyes, I don't look at it that way. You know the areas that need correcting, but you don't get them all wrong.*

The Lord wanted to spend time with me, and I blew it, but I don't always. Psalm 145:19 says, "He fulfills the desire of those who fear him: he hears their cry and saves them."

Sometimes it seems like a sacrifice to draw close to the Lord. It takes time and energy to come away with Him. When we do, though, peace and joy are found in His Presence.

A SOUND MIND AND FREEDOM FROM STRIFE

I read Joshua 21:43-45, "So the Lord gave Israel all the land He had sworn to give their forefathers, and they took possession of it and settled there. The Lord gave them rest on every side, just as He had sworn to their forefathers. Not one of their enemies withstood them; the Lord handed their enemies over to them. Not one of all the Lord's good promises to the house of Israel failed; everyone was fulfilled."

While I thought about how these verses on freedom from strife might apply to communicating without becoming angry, the Lord spoke:

A sound mind and freedom from strife are what I promised you. I have shown you the correct, righteous response to anger. Now is the time to search out the righteous responses to irritations. First and foremost, don't defend yourself.

INTO THE PROMISED LAND

Joshua spied out the Promised Land. He served as Moses' assistant and was trained under his leadership. Before Moses died, he appointed Joshua to be his replacement. When Joshua approached his own death, his words were, "Now I am about to go the way of all the earth" (Joshua 23:14). He assembled all the tribes of Israel at Shechem and challenged them to make a conscious choice to always serve God.

Joshua declared, "As for me and my household, we will serve the Lord" (Joshua 24:15).

In response, the Israelites declared to Joshua, "Far be it from us to forsake the Lord and serve other gods. It was God Himself who brought us and our fathers up out of Egypt, from the land of slavery. He protected us on our entire journey and among all the nations through which we traveled. The Lord drove out before all the nations including the Amorites who lived in the land. We too will serve the Lord, because He is our God. We will serve the Lord and obey Him (Joshua 24:16-18, 27).

Joshua sent the people away, each to his own inheritance, and Israel served the Lord through Joshua's lifetime. My study on Joshua was now complete.

God gave me instruction and a sound mind (2 Timothy 1:7). He showed me new ways of responding to my anger before speaking my thoughts. I may not have fully reached my "Promised Land" in this area, but I had learned many valuable lessons.

THE PAIN OF REJECTION

At the end of September, Krista was almost two and Brian was five months old. Often, in the midst of caring for them, I felt as though Mike rejected me, even though he did not. The Lord replied:

> *I have brought you to this place of emotional devastation so you would look to Me. I am rebuilding you emotionally, and I am also rebuilding your marriage communication. I will heal you of hurt and the sting of rejection. I will deaden the pain so you no longer sense it. You will not have an opportunity to feel rejection. I will train you to respond so differently that you will know it is Me intervening on your behalf. I am making you totally dependent on Me and not on any one person, including Mike.*

Watch Me work. Wait on Me early, and I will give you peace and a word in due season, during this period of frustration in your life. I will not leave you without hope in your emotions. HOPE will be My landmark even in emotional storms. I will minister to you at times when you are in despair. Trust me to do this mighty work in you. The rejection factor in your emotional make-up will be the last root to be dealt with.

REMINISCENCE OF BIBLE SCHOOL DAYS

Early in October, I read through the book of Ruth, especially chapters three and four.

The story in this book is an analogy of the work of Jesus. He is the Kinsman and Redeemer. Reading about Ruth reminded me of our Bible School days. The Lord said:

That place was a part of your spiritual heritage. The teachers helped you to grow up spiritually. Your time there gave you a new spiritual foundation and gave you a knowledge base about Me. Remember your first classes there? You soaked up all the knowledge about Me like a sponge. I caused you to hunger and thirst after Me. Look to Me, the Author and Finisher of your faith, and I will cause a new thing to well up in your being. It will burst forth in the right season, and you will begin to teach others about Me.

RETREAT REFLECTIONS

During the fall, I drove to a nearby retreat center for an overnight stay. Krista was almost two years old, and Brian turned five months old.

My mother called the evening before and said that she might have chronic lymphocytic leukemia. I was terrified and called a friend to pray for my mom and me.

When I arrived at the retreat center, I talked to one of the nuns. She also said that she would pray for me. I prayed, "Lord, please set Mom free from sickness."

Another nun came in to check on me. She was from India and was very kind. She said she was available to talk or pray with me.

While at the center, I took a writing break, had breakfast, and walked along a nature trail by the lake. Later, I began writing about various situations in my life.

Outwardly, I had everything that any Christian woman might want–a Christian husband and two healthy children. We were financially stable, so I did not have to work outside the home. I had asked Jesus into my life in 1977, and continued to walk with Him. I was actively involved in a Bible-believing church, yet, something was missing. "Lord, I pray that I will find fulfillment in You, however nebulous that sounds. I know that the answer is in You, Lord."

My focus turned to my mother and the illnesses she had struggled with during most of my growing up years, and I was angry. Who was I angry with? And what was I angry about? Was it God's will to have her miserable and unhealthy? I don't think so. Was it some form of manipulation to get attention? Yet, how can one produce heart disease which required a triple bypass surgery? Or stomach ulcers, pancreas inflammation, countless colds, pleurisy, pneumonia, bursitis in her elbows, lumps on her back, tear duct infections, glaucoma, cataracts, infection in her heart surgery incision, and now chronic lymphocytic leukemia? All of these things seemed too much for Mom to bear. My prayer became, "Lord, help me to see this with Your eyes."

The answer to some of these prayers came in a booklet I found in the prayer room entitled, "Suggested Scripture Passages for Prayer." The author said to pick a scripture passage, relax in God's Presence, and pray to the Holy Spirit for openness and guidance. Then, slowly, read the passage, pause when something strikes you, and let God lead you where He will. I read Psalm 23:2, "He leads me beside still waters. He restores my soul." Another version read, "You lead me to restful waters to restore my soul."

I believe there is far more to this walk with the Lord than I was experiencing, and I was on a quest to find maximum fulfillment and joy in my life. Although sometimes He takes us to a physical place like this retreat center, He always calls us to come away with Him. Our place of solitude can be right where we are, without having to travel.

On this personal retreat, I brought a stack of unanswered letters, four of my past journals in hopes of finding words from the Lord to highlight, two books, and the Peace music cassette tape. As I poured my heart, He spoke to my innermost thoughts:

Although you have a desire to accomplish these things, the time frame is off. The letters are good to send off. Listen to the cassette tape to quiet your soul. Find My words to you in the journals. Reflect on them and see how far I have led you. The books have good things, yet, reading and meditating on My Word is better.

All these things can be done in due season. But first, find Me, not just information about Me. I will come to you when you seek Me with all your heart. I will fill you up.

As for my relationship with Mike, the Lord impressed on me that our communication process can be developed. We are mates brought together by God. Instead of complaining, becoming reflective, or unduly introspective, I can meet Mike's needs and understand what makes him tick.

I asked the Lord about Krista and believe that He gave me some direction on her eating patterns. I am to leave her growth to the Lord. I am doing the best I know. She will let me know when she is hungry. The Lord said:

Capitalize on those times. Gradually she will fall into a predictable pattern. Choose healthy foods you know that she likes. Gradually introduce new foods. She will gain weight and grow. Mike is a partner to you in raising Krista and

Brian. He is balanced and level-headed in the things that concern you. He will help you break through your confusion about these issues.

Next, my thoughts in prayer turned to my mom.

I have called you to intercede for your mom's well-being, wholeness, and health. After each conversation, write down the issues that concern you, and then intercede for her.

During the summer, I talked to my parents numerous times, especially after Mom had her heart attack and open heart surgery. God asked me to pray for her, and stand in the gap between her and Satan for health.

When I arrived at the retreat center, my heart was heavy with many fears and anxieties. As I prayed, the Lord gave me insight. I returned home, knowing that God would carry me, and I could turn to Him anytime and anyplace. My soul was restored.

REJECTION

In October, I prayed about the rejection I had felt from certain people. The Lord spoke:

This is the time to deal effectively with rejection. This is what "forsake" means. It means to reject. I will never leave, forsake, or reject you. I want to be a personal God to you. Think of Me as your Father and husband. I will fulfill those roles for you.

I said, "Yes, Lord, but you don't have "skin" on. And He said,

Physical skin is not necessary. I will fulfill this spiritually by My Spirit. It is too complicated to explain in earthly terms, yet I will do it, and you will understand when I come to you in this way. I will heal you of the fear of rejection, as well as rejections in the past. You will change your view of people who rejected you. Conflict happened last night, but the resolution of these issues will bear the fruit of improved health and greater wholeness in you.

My response was, "Hallelujah!" Starting August 18, 1990, my watchword for the next year became, "Reconciliation with Mike." I believed reconciliation with Dad would be next.

OUT OF THE DARKNESS

During a sermon, the pastor spoke on Jesus, who is the Light in the darkness. He asked the congregation, "Are you in darkness?"

From his sermon, I wrote things to do when experiencing darkness:

1) *Don't listen to your feelings.*
2) *Choose to worship God.*
3) *Learn to worship God in the darkness.*
4) *Learn to spit in the Devil's eye by saying, "All the things you say about my life may be factually true, but I will still trust God. He is my strength."*

Next, the Lord spoke to me:

There is a way out of your present darkness—not out of your circumstances, or onto the mission field, or into a bigger house, or any other outward change. I will bring you through darkness to the other side where light will shine inside of you. Remember the children's book, Puppy Lost? *Krista was seventeen months old when your aunt bought that for her. Hold My hand, like the puppy held his mother's hand.*

EMOTIONALLY HEALED

Why am I depressed? Yesterday I had one set of problems, and now I have another. I feel caught in a web. One person said I may need psychological help. Is that even biblical? I need help, but would professional counseling be the right route? Shouldn't counseling be inside the church?

All I can say right now is, "Lord, please lead me concerning my feelings. Don't let me get caught up in the world's way of overcoming. I want to be led by You. Psychology and psychotherapy are worldly terms to me. Help me to break through all of this."

Last night Mike and I talked for two hours and had a breakthrough discussing many issues. "Thank You, Lord."

I sensed the Lord respond:

> *You will be healed emotionally as you raise Krista. A stable family unit and family life are important. What you do affects everyone else in the family. You are a team. Reach out to the neighborhood around you. Earn the right to be heard from the neighbor kids. Your children's first seven years are important. Basic behavior is learned early. Be a nonjudgmental friend. Control your behavior and vocabulary. Consider what Proverbs and the New Testament say about anger. Get the Living Bible and the New American Standard Versions of the Bible for additional insights and comparison.*

OVERWHELMING CIRCUMSTANCES

In early November, Dad called to say that Mom had another heart attack. Krista was two years old and had an ear infection. Brian was six months and had a temperature of 101.4. Both kids wanted my attention. The house was a mess. Bible study met that night and I had to make a cake. I felt overwhelmed. My aunt came over when I asked if she would help me.

Later, in my time alone, I looked into God's word for encouragement. I came through the day lighter in heart and grateful to the Lord and to my aunt, who came over and eased my load.

DIFFERENCE BETWEEN FEAR AND WORRY

One day, I studied Bible verses on fear and worry. These emotions were ones that I felt most frequently.

The definition of fear is:

- *An agitated feeling aroused by awareness of actual or threatened danger, trouble, dread, terror.*

- *An uneasy feeling that something may happen contrary to one's desire.*

- *An awe or reverence of God.*

- *A continuing state or attitude of fright, dread, or alarmed concern i.e. to live in fear.*

The definition of worry is:

- *A state of anxiety or vexation.*
- *To feel anxiety about something. To fret.*
- *To be uneasy in the mind.*
- *Cares.*

My prayer that day was that God would give me contentment. He replied:

Your ministry for now is to care for these little ones and listen to Me.

When He spoke these words, I relaxed, because I didn't sense the pressure to do anything more that day. His yoke is easy and His burden is light.

GOD IS YOUR MARRIAGE COUNSELOR

When I sat down to journal, read the Bible, and pray later that day, God spoke to me about our marriage:

This is the counsel you have been looking for. It is with Me. First of all, don't complain or nag about your relationship with Mike. Be humble. When the choice is in front of you, take the "humble seat." Be gracious. Place Mike first and fit into his plans. Lay your expectations on the altar. Take the path of least resistance. Don't share your struggles in detail with others. Allow Me to change you. Bring Mike's needs before Me, and leave them there. Give him first choice with what he would like to do with the kids, and which of you is to watch them. Your place is in the home right now, whether you like it at times, or not. You really wouldn't enjoy it any other way. Believe Me!

Look at keys for your marriage in other books I lead you to. Don't concentrate on how Mike should change, but on how I can change you and your attitudes.

You are doing fine. You are not off your rocker. It is high time for you to believe that. You are normal and of a sound mind. The world may tell you about characteristic patterns of your past, and you may even line up with them, reject their label. I am the Deliverer, and I alone have the authority to do a deep inner cleansing to change the thought patterns that were established long before you ever knew Me.

I am also the Lord of the past. It is behind you. If you see a trait that does not line up with what My will for you, leave it to Me to change you. I will cause you to line up to the person I created you to be, which is to be free in Me. I made you and love your very nature.

You will begin to unfold like a flower. Your fragrance like the uncorked glass bottle with the flower in it that was given to you, will be evident to all. It is time to release the fragrance of Christ. "Uncork the top" was what your friend said before she died.

Remember 2 Corinthians 2:15-16 says, "For we are to God the aroma of Christ among those who are being saved and those who are perishing. To the one we are the smell of death; to the other, the fragrance of life."

Think of the verse in the hymn, "Come Thou Fount" that says, "Here's my heart; O, take and seal it, seal it for Thy courts above." Don't be driven by your flesh. Rest in Me. When I tell you to rest, then REST. Don't be busy, just to be busy. You will have ample time to do the important things. Whatever happens, I allow it.

I was amazed at how encouraging and freeing God's words were to me. They were life to me, more than any counseling session, because He is the Counselor.

HEARTFELT PRAYER

I couldn't sleep in the middle of the night because of a sore throat, so I took an over the counter medication for it. I prayed, "Lord, please give me freedom from my self-centered life and way of thinking. Please give me joy in every circumstance and situation. I want contentment. I want to be patient, gentle, loving, kind, merciful, joyful, peaceful, long-suffering, and self-controlled."

Then, I read Galatians 5 and personalized it. I am to love Mike as I love myself. Instead of loving him, I often find myself being critical, malicious, spiteful, full of bitterness, and holding onto grudges.

"Lord, deliver me from this nature."

I noted Proverbs 29:11, "A fool gives full vent to his anger, but a wise man keeps himself under control." Also, Proverbs 2:28 says, "Like a city whose walls are broken down is a man who lacks self-control."

Remember, Bonnie, do not be a quarrelsome wife.

I read these scriptures in other Bible translations. By this time, my sore throat was gone, and I went off to bed with a refreshed soul and spirit.

I WILL SEE YOU THROUGH THIS

On November 20, while pondering the trials that have overwhelmed me in my life, the Lord said:

I will see you through this.

My response was, "Hallelujah! You are wonderful, Lord. You are healing me! You are giving me unspeakable joy." The Lord impressed these words in my mind:

I'm causing you to trust Me, even in the darkness. Hold My hand as a daughter holds onto the hand of a loving fa-

ther. *You will sense and even know the Father heart of God through your earthly father. This is the year of reconciliation with Mike. Next year, August 18, 1991, will begin the year of reconciliation with your dad. Now, enjoy life. Enjoy reading for enjoyment.*

"Hallelujah!" I responded again. "Thank You, Lord."

I reread in Stormie Omartian's book and focused on a portion in which she explained how a dream had revealed her unforgiveness toward her father.[11] I asked, "What does this have to do with me, Lord?"

I sensed Him say:

There are specific deliverances and answers to prayer for specific healings. I have the keys to set you free. All you have to do is ask! I will bring you to greater depths of prayer and communion with Me. Be obedient to Me when in doubt. Ask Me for clarity and truth. Have confidence in this. Begin with prayer for specific areas of freedom.

Mike is to be part of this. You will grow together in this area of prayer. Your ministry as a team will blossom and flower. The fruit of it will be evident to all. As I spoke to you in 1987, I speak again now to give you hope. You will not be forgotten. Your place in My kingdom will be one of great honor, once you lay down your life to be a servant to all.

I love you, Mike, and your children. You will be a blessing and a greater joy to Me. My timing is key here. Hang on to My words which will not return to Me void. Read, Streams in the Desert. Times of refreshing are here for you in the wilderness, even when nothing changes outwardly. As you rest in Me and are refreshed by times such as these, you will see My deliverance for you, and a way through the valley of the shadow of death.

---

[11] Stormie Omartian, *Stormie*, 4th ed. (Eugene, OR: Harvest House Publishers, 1989), 161.

At this time, I read more about Stormie's life, about her unforgiveness toward her father.[12] She had grown up to distrust all male authority, which was manifested by extreme independence. After she received prayer, was anointed with oil, and forgave the specific males in her life, she was set free.

Her experience reminded me of the counseling Mike and I received from the pastor before Krista was conceived. My prayer was, "Lord, show me any unforgiveness toward any family members. Once I recognize it, show me what to do, and help me to be obedient so deliverance can come."

Many experiences came to mind, and I asked God for the ability to forgive, and to let go of my past unforgiveness. Peace flowed like a river. Over time, I also needed to ask for forgiveness of individuals as God led the way.

REASON FOR ANGER

Mike, Krista, Brian, and I went out for ice cream that same night and had a great time. Suddenly, Mike gave Krista (age two) the steak knife to lick off the ice cream. It shocked me. I became angry at him, and I couldn't talk about it.

During my time with the Lord later that night, I wrote in my journal. "Lord, why did I become so angry with Mike when he handed Krista a steak knife to lick off the ice cream?"

He said:

Anyone could have given Krista the steak knife, and you would have been angry with them. The issue is not the person, but the situation. Separate the situation from the person. You and I will work on this until you have it conquered. Your rage will subside.

---

[12]Ibid., 162.

"Thank You, Lord." This helped me to be less angry at Mike. I explained to him how I feared that she might cut her mouth or tongue. He hadn't thought about that; he only wanted her to taste the ice cream. We had such different points of view. Ugh!

WHEN CLOUDS APPEAR, TAKE COVER IN JESUS

During my quiet time, I prayed, "Lord, in my reading today, could You give me a glimpse of what all my inner turmoil is about? Why am I so shaken today? Why am I struggling so? Why am I so insecure again about Mike and me?"

Be thankful and grateful. You have a lot going for you. Watch the clouds, and when they start to appear, take cover in Jesus. Do not go out without an umbrella of His covering. The Lord gave David victory everywhere he went. You'll have victory, too. Focus on Me. Conflicts can produce growth. You are not yet on the other side. That is why you feel so uncomfortable. You will make it through and praise Me in the end. Your rebellion is going to be a stench in Mike's nostrils, as well as mine. Lay it down. I'll show you what to do.

God directed me to read about Absalom's rebellion in 2 Samuel 8:13-14, 2 Samuel 12:14, and 1 Chronicles 18:12-13.

I experienced a greater peace and hope in my relationship with Mike. I know that all couples struggle. With every victory and peace after every spat, I communicate better through the next trial.

PLAGUES OF GOD OR SATAN

In mid-December, I read in 2 Samuel 24:1-17 and 1 Chronicles: 1-30, that King David took a census of Israel. Why would this be such a bad thing? Perhaps David was too proud of his mighty army or relied too much on them. In any case, this did not please God, and He gave David a choice of three punishments: three years of famine, three months of fleeing from his enemies, or three days of plague in his land. He chose the last of the three evils, and the Lord sent a plague on Israel that caused 70,000 of Israel's men to fall dead before God asked the angel to withdraw his hand.

In my journal I wrote about my own "plagues." Krista and I had pink eye, Brian had a cold, and Mike's allergies flared up. I asked the Lord if there was a reason why we were plagued with illness. Were we doing something wrong? If so, I prayed that God would show us. Was this just the plague of illness typical to young families? I thought health was mine in Jesus' name. Or, did these illnesses happen to produce endurance and increase our characters?

The verses that stood out in today's readings were 1 Chronicles 22:19- 20, "Now, devote your heart and soul to seeking the Lord, your God. Begin to build the sanctuary of the Lord."

I felt impressed that the Lord said to me:

Mike and Bonnie, take heed to the words in Psalm 30.

In Psalm 30 I read, "...O Lord my God, I called to You for help and You healed me...You turned my wailing into dancing; you removed my sackcloth and clothed me with joy, that my heart may sing to You and not be silent. O Lord my God, I will give You thanks forever."

As I looked back on these circumstances, I realized that I can still have joy in the Lord by making a choice, even though everyone in our house endured sickness. Were these hardships from Satan? I never knew for sure, but I did end up rejoicing in the Lord, which I know pleased Him. And for that, I felt more settled.

PAINFUL MEMORY HEALED

In church on Sunday, I took sermon notes. The pastor said, "Mistakes aren't planned. No one would make them if they were. But we do make them. We all make mistakes. Sometimes they are for a necessary purpose. Mistakes humble us, and sometimes lead to the healing of memories."

While I played piano for praise and worship that day, I made a mistake. I started to play the wrong song. The music leader stopped me in front of the entire church, and I was quickly able to get back on track with the correct song. Yet, I felt humiliated that it happened.

Suddenly, a memory from twenty years before flashed in my mind. I had played piano for our high school choir's performance in a state music contest. The judges sat right in front of the choir. In the pressure of the situation, I lost my place in the music. As I continued to play, the choir director tried to tell me where we were in the music but, I couldn't hear her. All I saw was her stern look and the angry eyes of the choir members fixed on me. I began to make more mistakes and felt horrible and sick inside.

On the bus back to school, there were plenty of empty seats, but no one sat next to me. I felt rejected. I didn't know the Lord then. I wanted to have someone near to comfort me and tell me it was okay. Yet no one did.

The flashback of my high school experience had stayed with me, and the pain of that experience seemed ever-present.

When I made the mistake in church, I sensed all eyes were on me, and tears flowed as I began to play the correct hymn. A lady from church came up and put her arms around me. She didn't say a word, but her touch, like the Lord touching me through her, healed both painful mistakes. Her loving hug declared that everything was okay and healing tears were like the balm from Gilead.

Later, I asked the Lord, "Where were You when I played piano in high school and where were You at church when I played? I made terrible mistakes."

He lovingly replied:

I was with you both times. I was next to you on the piano bench, on the bus seat next to you as you rode home, and today I hugged you through Nancy. It is okay to make mistakes. Your value is not in what you do. I will catch you when you fall. I will heal you of painful memories, so you no longer sense the sting of them as you look back.

COME AWAY WITH ME

As I read in 1 Samuel 18:1-4 about David's friendship with Jonathan, a new song came to mind, I had never received a song from the Lord before. As I wrote the words, the melody came with it.

COME AWAY WITH ME
Come away! Come away! Come away from the world.
Cling to Me. Cling to Me. I'll set you free
From the bonds of the world till at last you're with me.
There you'll stay in the cleft of the Rock amidst the storm.
When the storm has passed and the rainbow appears
You'll remember my covenant to you.
No storm will flood you out,
But above it you will rise.
I'm the Ark, I'm the One. You'll be safe inside me.

Let it go, let it go, all the cares, all the world.

All the struggles, all the pain, don't hold it in.
Though the mountains be shaken
And the hills are removed.
Yet my unfailing love for you will not be shaken.
Nor my covenant of peace shall not be removed,
Says the Lord, Who has compassion on you.

I'll cling to you as a closest friend.

You can rest your soul on me, and I'll commune with you.
I won't leave or forsake you
Or desert you in times of need.
My faithfulness and love I'll pour out on you.
Your security in the world will all pass away.

Yet, I'm your defense and security in the world.
So cling to Me and you won't be disappointed.
I'll teach you what a friend should be.
But hold worldly friends loosely.
My purposes of friends, even friends in Me will pre-
vail.
Yet hold them loosely, as I may see need to move them
on.
However, I will not leave you empty-handed,
As I will meet your need for true communion,
And as I see fit, I will bring friends into your life
To enhance your walk with me.
Come away! Come away! Come away with Me
Here you'll stay, here you'll stay
You'll abide safe in Me.
I will love you with an everlasting love
Unconditional love, and faithful love.
Here I'll stay by your side.
You will rest safe in Me.
Turn your back on the world,
no place to be,
For a lifelong friend in Me only you will find.
I'll love you as you've never been loved before.
For a lifelong friend in Me only you will find.
I'll love you as you've never been loved before.

FINDING YOUR PLACE IN GOD

Our Sunday school class at church studied the spiritual gifts. Each of us took some written tests to determine our spiritual giftings. God said:

I'm having you take these tests in order for you to see how I've created you. You are unique, different, and come with special gifting for My purposes. I'll be the One to tell you what to do in this life. Finding your place sometimes involves tests and personal prophesies. I will spell out your ministry.

FRIENDS FROM THE PAST

Mike and I went to a bed and breakfast place for some much needed quiet time, while an aunt watched our children. As I contemplated a few old friends, names came to mind. God showed me the place that each had in my life and said:

> Look at Proverbs 21:14 about giving a gift in secret. Sending out newsletters and pictures is like giving a gift in secret.

He gave me names of people I hadn't seen for some years and I sent newsletters to them. He added:

> They were a part of your life once and led to your spiritual growth.

Some responded, and others didn't. Yet the cards I received in return felt like gifts returned and I felt blessed.

ENCOURAGEMENT

In April, I went to a women's retreat. After a wonderful teaching, I posed a question to myself: What things would I want to hear from others to be encouraged? I wrote,

- *"You hear from the Lord."*
- *"You are a good mother and homemaker."*
- *"I appreciate you as a friend.*
- *You have something of worth to offer the body of Christ.*
- *It doesn't matter that you don't currently work as a nurse practitioner.*

God also spoke to me:

> You are important to me and you are doing what I've called you to do and be.

I believe that these words were a gift from the Lord and what I wanted to hear for encouragement.

PREPARING FOR THE TRIP TO CHICAGO

In early May, I visited a friend in Chicago. She had traveled with me to Uganda in 1983. The day before my trip, these words came:

The Spirit goes before you for the trip ahead. Don't be afraid about what to say. My Spirit goes before you to prepare another's heart for a mighty encounter with the Living God. She will come to know Me in a most interesting and exciting way. Hands off. Let Me do this work.

During the trip, these words encouraged me after a time of emotional weariness:

This break in your daily routine is from Me to give you peace and rest, so that you can be refreshed to face the normal trials and tribulations at home. Have no fear. Remember what your friend said, "My plan is to bring you to the eye of the storm and keep you there." I will never give you more than you can handle.

Keep your eyes on Me. Run to Me often in your heart. I will cover and protect you. Seek Me when you don't know which way to turn. Seek Me early in the storm. Then I'll give you protection to walk straight through it to the eye in the storm.

I'll keep you safe from the hand of the enemy that seeks to destroy your marriage and rob your peace and joy. He can only succeed if you give him ground by turning his way instead of toward Me. Choose Me in every trial and tribulation, and follow the way I guide you to walk through these things. Your peace will return, and your marriage will be a lasting one—not only one that endures, but one that will be a shining example to others, and a fulfilling one for you. This is only possible as you walk in My ways instantly in every situation. I will give you your heart's deepest desires.

Set Me at the highest place in your life, and I won't let you be disappointed, or deny you the peace and joy in marriage that you desire. It will be a blending of Mike's heart and yours as one in body, soul, and spirit. You've longed for it. You've prayed that this will be a godly and upright marriage. I've heard your cries for help. Seek Me alone and together. Put Me above all else in your lives. Live wholly for Me every step of the way. I hold you in the palm of My hand. I never will leave you. Repent and make things right, as the case may be, so you once again have joyous fellowship with Me and with one another.

This trip is for your enjoyment. Be wise in your spending. I'll lead the way. I go before you.

BAD ATTITUDES

At the end of May, these words came to me:

Morning has broken, as the song writer states, yet you have not broken.

I asked, "In what way, Lord?"

You are still carrying a grudge towards your friend at church. My ways are not yours in handling this matter. Do not stuff your hurts and disappointments. They are meant to be dealt with but only as you allow Me to be the Healer. Talk with her. Get it out in the open. Names do not have to be mentioned, but the negative attitude that was passed on from one person to you by phone was evident to all. Remember, that person is responsible to Me for her attitudes of criticism and judgment. Her thoughts, words, and deeds are My responsibility to judge, not yours. Release her to Me.

You are responsible to Me alone. Come to Me. Mike can be a big help to you in discerning these matters. That will draw you closer together as you share your reactions to matters with him. He will feel helpful and needed by you. You, in turn, will be able to better judge how to respond to people who caused you disappointment and hurt, even if it is only perceived by you.

Hold on to the promises I gave you yesterday morning as you read in Isaiah 51. They will come to pass. I will refresh you, but not in the way you think. Removal from the situation will not cause refreshment, but the little oasis of times with Me from which you'll draw your strength. They will bring refreshment by My spirit and My living water. Drink freely.

Buy a separate notebook for the songs that give you life. Place them in a three-ring notebook with divisions. Record your goals.

I did each of these things, and in obeying, I found joy.

LIKE A PRECIOUS RAG DOLL

On June 24, I settled our kids for a nap and took the phone off the hook. I napped as well. When I woke up, the kids were still asleep. I heard "precious rag doll" in my mind and sensed that the Lord had a word for me. I also knew there was something about a porcelain doll, and yet knew the word was to start with a rag doll. I wrote what the Lord brought to mind:

Like a precious rag doll that has been discarded in the corner, battered, abused, used, then thrown away, I found you, dusted you off, and hugged you ever so gently, lovingly. I carried you with me wherever I went, and slowly, but surely, you healed. You needed sewing, and re-stuffing where parts of you had lost substance. Your eye needed re-sewing. Your dress and other clothes were tattered and torn, and badly in need of repair. I removed these, not to expose your nakedness to the public, but to replace your clothing with a beautiful white, satin dress, like a bride getting ready for her bridegroom to carry her off to the bridal-chamber.

Your face shows signs of many tears, yet I wipe them away and replace your Raggedy Ann head with a fine porcelain head, with a fair and new face and bright shining eyes to replace the red, worn, and broken buttons. Your mouth, which had permanent sadness to its shape, will be uplifted in a very wide smile to show your beautiful white teeth. Instead of your Raggedy Ann black button nose, yours will be beautifully shaped, and graceful in its curve. Your fine ivory complexion encompasses it all. You have long arms, long slender legs, and beautifully manicured nails completing the long slender fingers on each hand. And you will wear gold rings, sapphires, diamonds, emeralds, and rubies, the same jewels that crown your head. Your hair is like silk. It is no longer red yarn tied in braids, but golden locks perfectly in place beneath your white veil.

Oh, my lovely bride. No longer are you like a little girl, but now you are a grown woman, maturing for her bridegroom. Come away, my beloved, to My inner chambers and I will tenderly love you. You are My very own. I will never leave or forsake you, but give to you joys forevermore. Drink of Me freely. All that I have, I give to you. Nevermore despairing, nevermore in want, you will find your needs will be fulfilled to a greater extent than you ever dreamed possible.

Love me, My darling, gentle one. Your nature is very pleasing to Me. I created you for loving. I created you for Myself. And you will know fulfillment and joy within My Presence.

If ever you feel discarded and used like an old rag doll, come to Me and I will transform you into a beautiful porcelain doll, yet alive, living and breathing for Me. I will revive you. I will nurture and care for you. I will cherish and love you as you have never been loved before. Bonnie, My sweet, lovely one.

I closed my journal, and sat in awe as I quietly praised my God: "Glory, glory, glory to the King. I stand before my King well adorned in robes of righteousness and truth."

WORD CONFIRMED IN THE BIBLE

The next day, June 25, I read the "Bible in a Year" passage for the day, which was Ezekiel 16:4-14. These scriptures beautifully confirmed the word I had received from the Lord the previous day:

> ⁴On the day you were born your cord was not cut, nor were you washed with water to make you clean, nor were you rubbed with salt or wrapped in cloths.⁵No one

looked on you with pity or had compassion enough to do any of these things for you. Rather, you were thrown out into the open field, for on the day you were born you were despised.

6"'Then I passed by and saw you kicking about in your blood, and as you lay there in your blood I said to you, "Live!"7I made you grow like a plant of the field. You grew and developed and entered puberty. Your breasts had formed and your hair had grown, yet you were stark naked.

8"'Later I passed by, and when I looked at you and saw that you were old enough for love, I spread the corner of my garment over you and covered your naked body. I gave you my solemn oath and entered into a covenant with you, declares the Sovereign Lord, and you became mine.

9"'I bathed you with water and washed the blood from you and put ointments on you.10 I clothed you with an embroidered dress and put sandals of fine leather on you. I dressed you in fine linen and covered you with costly garments.11I adorned you with jewelry: I put bracelets on your arms and a necklace around your neck, 12 and I put a ring on your nose, earrings on your ears and a beautiful crown on your head.13So you were adorned with gold and silver; your clothes were of fine linen and costly fabric and embroidered cloth. Your food was honey, olive oil and the finest flour. You became very beautiful and rose to be a queen.14 And your fame spread among the nations on account of your beauty, because the splendor I had given you made your beauty perfect, declares the Sovereign Lord.

Though these verses figuratively describe Israel's beauty as a nation and her unfaithfulness, the Lord's care for Israel in making and saving her paralleled the word I received from the Lord the day before. I believe this describes believers as well and was blessed to know how tenderly God loves and cares for us.

KEYS TO A RENEWED MARRIAGE

When one of my uncles died, I flew to Bismarck, North Dakota for his funeral. On the return flight to Minneapolis, I talked with a cousin who was on the same flight. I learned he was a Christian. We talked about many things, including marriage. He asked,

"Are you really committed to your marriage?"

"Yes," I replied.

"Do you know what the stresses are in Mike's job?"

"No, I don't, not really."

"That is sad to say. Take an interest in him. Find out about Mike—not just what his day was like, but WHAT was in his day to like or not like. How is he feeling? Give one hundred per cent of your attention to him when he comes home. Your marriage comes first, then the kids."

All of this was good advice. On the plane home, I prayed, "Lord, Mike and I need more time to cultivate our marriage and make it stronger. Please point the way. Show us the next step. We need to have a more Christ-centered marriage for a stronger marriage bond.

Then, the Lord spoke:

I long for you to have a better relationship with Mike. I have heard your cries for help. Keep close to Me, and I'll tell you what to do, and when, in this life.

Yes, you will write, but My timing and purposes will prevail. I love you, My child. I'm your Father. I will be close by your side. There will be ones like your cousin who will teach you. They are My gifts to you. Learn from them. They have something to offer of worth and value. So do you. My Spirit of love and gentleness is in you. You have great worth in My sight. You need to see this. You have worth as a person that I've created. I will open your eyes to see this, but in a way so that you can receive it with humility.

181

Bless you, My child. Go forward in peace and joy in My Spirit. You are exuberant and radiant today. Mike will be glad.

CHANGE OF HEART

On August 4, our small group leader at church asked if he could come over to speak with us about an issue, and he stayed for over two hours. He commented about not needing to study a book in the Bible, as all of us have Bible knowledge, so we don't have to take the time to study the Bible in a group setting. My interpretation of what he said disturbed me. This man, also an elder at the church, didn't seem to think that studying the Bible was important. He said that times of praising the Lord and worshiping until 1:00 a.m. are from a bygone era. When I asked him what era he was into now, he said,

"I'm into good works now."

There is truth about caring for widows and orphans in need. This is true religion. James 1:27 says, "Religion that our Father accepts as pure and faultless is this: to look after orphans and widows in their distress and to keep oneself from being polluted by the world."

I consider my inward walk with God to be a vital part of my life, a springboard for everything else I do. When my small group leader expressed that Bible study and an inward walk with God were a small part of his life, and that doing good works was more important, I had a hard time accepting his leadership.

In September, another church elder taught a class on parenting, which Mike and I attended. By doing so, we left the small group led by the other elder.

Sometimes, Mike and I struggled with thoughts of leaving our church. This was certainly a change of heart for us. So much had been invested in relationships and music ministry during the years there.

After the parenting class, Mike and I planned to re-evaluate our place at this church. God is our guide and will light our path as we seek Him for direction.

WANTING ANSWERS

I woke up at 2:00 a.m. August 9, with heaviness in my heart. I prayed: "Lord, help me to make sense of our small group meeting last evening. No one seemed to care about the Holy Spirit conference I attended, yet it was life-giving for me. How I long to hear Your discernment about what went on. I'm upset and grieved over what took place. Lord, it is not helping me to mull this over in my mind. I can't hear You. Yet, I wait for You to speak words of truth to my heart."

Later that morning, I sensed the Lord say,

I am leading you out. Don't be concerned about what other people think. You must not hold unforgiveness or bitterness towards anyone in the group.

But I do, Lord. I confess this to You. Please work in my heart.

I know your need for intimate fellowship, but it will be with those who have made me Lord in their life and desire deeper things. I have called you to a higher walk, to things above the earth, and not to be tangled with things below. The cares of this world will only choke you and place Me outside your life. I don't want that for you. I have invested in you and deposited My Holy Spirit in you for a greater work in My Kingdom.

Don't be dismayed by My workings in this church. Don't tangle yourself in it. Let it go! I will have you give a word in due season, but it will be a life-giving word, and not one that produces a death blow to the church. I am a God of restoration, not one who stomps the life out of sinners! There are those that would scoff at this word and how you hear and discern My voice. Pay no attention to that. I do speak to you and you hear Me in this way. I will lead you to others who have this kind of walk as well. Deep calls to deep. Let those who desire shallowness and surface relationships be for themselves. It is not for you.

I have placed within you a desire for deep fellowship with others, as you have with Me. It is not for self-glorification but to pray, edify each other, and build each other up in the Body of Christ, in order to be empowered by My Spirit to do a great work in My kingdom.

At this point, I had a vision of a football game and players (whom I learned later from Mike were called blockers or line men) who were broad-shouldered. These players keep the opposing team away from the player who is running with the ball, so he can reach the goal line.

Then the Lord spoke to me of my calling in this life,

You are to be the one who protects others from enemies who try to keep them from reaching the goal that God has in mind for them. You are to encourage the one with the ball to run and keep going towards the goal. You are to stand in the gap between them and Satan. You are to fight for them through prayer and do battle in the Spirit by prayer for them. This is My purpose for you in this life.

My Church needs great encouragement. It is for those who hear My voice who long for Me. Let the dead bury their own dead. I have called you into life and will lead you every step of the way. Don't be concerned that you couldn't hear My voice right away last night. There was a deep spiritual warfare taking place. You were still in the midst of battle in the heavenlies until now. You are now released, but before there was a pull to keep you. They are not wrong where they are. That is up to Me to see that they are in the place I have for them. I have a different place for you. You are released. You are set free! Rejoice in Me. The chains are off. Set the captives free as well. You are bought with the price of My blood on Calvary. Rejoice!

MARRIAGE TO THE LORD

I drove to my favorite place along White Bear Lake, just a few minutes from our home. This time I sat by a tree and thought of the tree described in Psalm 1 which represents the life of those who seek God. Psalm 1:3 compares them to a tree planted by streams of water, which yields fruit in due season, and whose leaf does not wither. Whatever he does prospers.

Jeremiah 17:7 says, "Blessed is the man who trusts in the Lord, whose confidence is in him. He will be like a tree planted by the water that sends out its roots by the stream. It does not fear when heat comes; its leaves are always green. It has no worries in a year of drought and never fails to bear fruit."

I also wrote about marriage. Marriage is to be a delight, joy of all joys, rejoicing in the wife or husband of your youth. Isaiah 62:4 says, No longer will they call you Deserted, or name your land Desolate. But you will be called Hephzibah,[13]and your land Beulah[14]; for the Lord will take delight in you, and your land will be married. Then, the Lord spoke to me:

> *My delight is in you, Bonnie, just as you are. I see you not as you wish you were, but just as you are. Your marriage is to parallel your marriage to Me. It is not perfect, but will be perfect with Me, and as a bridegroom rejoices over his bride, so will I rejoice over you.*

---

[13] *Hephzibah* means *my delight is in her.*

[14] *Beulah* means *married.*

WRONG ATTITUDES TOWARD PEOPLE

I listened to the sermon in church and began to think about relationships with past church members. Sometimes, I held grudges. When I switched churches, I still carried grudges. I prayed, "Lord help me to stop that pattern." He said,

> I am a God of Restoration. I will give a word in due season and it will be a life-giving word, and not one that produces a death blow to the church.

Then, He gave me an assignment, which I worked on all afternoon. I started at the top of a blank page and listed each person who came to mind. I wrote about any hurts I felt from that person, any grudge I had toward that person, and how I saw that individual. I prayed for each one.

Next, I moved on from one person to another that God brought to mind, praying until I had peace in my heart. The burden lifted.

GOD'S HEALING HIS WAY

During the night on August 19, I thought about my friends and I heard these words:

Let the dust settle.

Okay, Lord, I'm listening.

Trust Me to complete the work I began in you. It is not Your responsibility to fix all the pieces. I will lead you step by step to LIFE and your part in the puzzles of your life.

I will bring people in your path. Be patient. My timing is slower than yours, but perfect. I see your need for a deep healing even from your childhood and before, yet to dig up something not directed by Me, or out of My timing, will only lead you astray. Be discerning and cautious. Trust Me when I say, Don't get involved. Keep close to Me and listen to My instructions. The people I have put in your path are for your blessing and protection. I have invested My Spirit in them to lead you and others to My truth and help you in the process of discerning My ways. Don't go to the left or to the right.

You are very angry. I'll help to dispel the cause of your anger and direct it to the source. Listen for cues. I will lead you to uncover these things. Out of a heart of love for others you will be moved to help those around you.

Right now, your heart is covered with thorns, and because of those, your heart has grown calloused and hardened. As I remove the thorns and allow you to heal properly, the callousness will disappear because it will not need to protect itself against the piercing thorns. Once the thorns and calluses are removed, your heart will beat in a fuller way. Don't try to remove the thorns by yourself. You'll only pierce your fingers and bleed. Let Me pull out the thorns.

I asked, "What are the thorns?

Thorns are the cares of this world, cares of the church, your rejection of others, abuse of your skills and talents, insensitive people, demands of children, demands of Mike and the housework, and others you are not even aware of. Let Me remove them.

Let Me work within the small group to bring about My healing, workings, and ways. It is not your concern what others will do. Bring your concerns to Me. Then, leave them there.

Your friend will have the key for this issue on anger. She understands you emotionally. Give her a call and she will help you discern this word and what you are reading about regarding anger. You are not as far as your friend, regarding her understanding of anger, but don't be too harsh on yourself for not being in a higher place. You'll make it. These lessons are designed for you to learn discernment and take time, as you are doing now, to hear My voice on these issues. You are on My narrow path for you. Don't be dismayed by the ups and downs. I hold you by the hand, pick you up when you fall, and give you hugs when you need them. Rest when you need to for the long climb ahead, as Much Afraid did, in Hannah Hurnard's book, Hind's Feet in High Places.[15] *She had a similar journey. I am leading you to a higher plateau. The word through your friend is true. It will be a climb but the feasting available when you reach the top is worth it. I will be there at the marriage feast, ready and waiting for you. Hold on. This life is but a breath away from the True Lamb, and union of the Lamb and Bride.*

---

[15]Hannah Hurnard, *Hind's Feet on High Places* (Wheaton Illinois, Tyndale House Publishers, Inc., 1977).

This world is passing away. Hold on to things of eternal value. You have relationships to maintain, but anytime you sense heaviness about calling or writing, let it go. I will tell you when to call or write. My yoke is easy and my burden is light. Wait until the load is easier and I place a lightness and desire in you to call or write. Don't dig yourself into a hole and cover up. Go about your daily life, and you'll be surprised at how quickly the burdens will lift. Hold fast to My words. They will become life to you, both My written word, especially the New Testament readings and words of prophecy through others, and the words that I have given to you. Receive these words with faith that they are from Me. Obey what I say in them, as I will direct your steps.

Don't stay still when I tell you to walk. This is also My voice. Heed the unrest when you've become disobedient to me. Rest when I say rest, for you need to do this, too. Move when I tell you to move for your own sake to get out of danger. There is nothing wrong with your relationships as they are. Keep close to Me. I won't lead you astray but will lead you into right relationships, right standing with them and with Me. My voice is calling you. Lay the burdens down. It is time for sleep. Put your pen down and go to bed.

I did just that and I slept more soundly with peace in my heart.

GOD CHANGES FEELINGS

While the kids napped on August 29, I spent time praying and writing in my journal, even while my mind was filled with jealousy, strife, rejection, and other emotions. I heard the Lord say:

Keep your eyes focused on Me. As you allow Me to fulfill your needs for true fellowship, the jealousy and the rejection will leave. Bitterness and anger is not your portion. Release those feelings to Me. Your willingness to lay them down is the first step. The next step is My part to change your feel-

ings of rejection, anger, and jealousy, to ones of love, respect, and nurturing. It will not be in your power to muster these up. Confess the bad to Me. Let it go. Yearn for My will and heart and I will do the rest. The meeting will be fruitful. Now, rest in Me.

"Lord, help me to see the person that I am meeting today through Your eyes. Love her through me."

The Lord was with me when I met this lady, and all went smoothly. I shared my feelings without becoming angry. I listened more than I talked. Thank You Lord!

HOSPITALITY AND LOVE

Shortly before my relatives came to visit in September, the Lord spoke to my heart:

Show your relatives hospitality and love while they are here. This will be a glorious life-giving day if you continually look to Me, the Source of all life and pure joy. I want to fill you today with overflowing life.

Apologize to Krista, Mike and Brian for your impatience last night and not laying down your life for them.

Trust Me with the van. My timing to get a newer van will come. You will know which one by the peace you experience in your heart in an unhurried atmosphere and also by confirmation from others with no time pressure. It will fall in your lap as a gift from Me. You don't need to work so hard for it. Rest in Me and trust Me.

DON'T FOCUS ON PROBLEMS

On September 13, the Lord spoke to my heart:

Don't focus on your problems today. You will sink further in misery. Seek counsel about Krista, yet, don't give in to worry or fear. I will help you with your emotions. Thank you for being obedient to Me during this time.

I HAVE CALLED YOU BY NAME

When a church nearby held special meetings with a guest speaker, Mike and I attended. During one of the meetings, these words came to me:

I have called you by name. You are bought with a price. I created you for Me and I love you with an everlasting love. All I want is you. Healing is for you as is love, joy and life. You are a beautiful sight to behold, My lovely bride. You are adorned in white, holy, righteous, and pure before Me. You are innocent and clean, like a bride on her wedding day. Let your heart melt with My love for you. Linger here in My Presence. I see you through the blood of My Son. I find you worthy because of the death and resurrection of My Son.

I could hardly imagine that God sees me that way, and that He loves me so much, yet I know it is true. I went home that night with peace in my heart.

FOCUS IN ON ME

During the pre-service prayer time, these words came to me:

Focus on Me. Don't be dismayed at My working in this church. I am pleased with your efforts to approach Me and seek My face. Now, as I speak to you, don't harden your heart or ignore My prodding for you to do work in My Kingdom. The Pearl of Great Price is buried in this field. Excavate it. Display the pearl. Show the world that Jesus is that Pearl. He paid His life for you and the world. This message has been forgotten in the shuffle of "busy-ness." Put Him back in the place of highest honor that He deserves. Lift Him up for all the world to see. As He is lifted up, He will draw all men unto Himself.

A MIGHTY SHAKING

Mid-October, was a time of upheaval in my emotions. Krista was not quite three years old. Brian was about one and a half years old. I struggled with depression, yet I clung to the Lord. These words came to me,

There will be a mighty shaking like Jesus chasing out the money changers from the temple. My truth and right-eousness will prevail. My light will shine in every corner of darkness. Every stone will be overturned. Every person who remains will be exposed for the evil in their heart, not pub-licly, for only I know human hearts. For those who desire it, I will point out the error in their hearts. Compare it to the truth in My word. I require repentance and the shaking off of the old, unclean, and religious spirit.

I will require obedience to My Holy Spirit for those who desire to rule and reign with Me. If you choose life, know this, that there will be a mighty shaking, but it will make you glad. Justice will be done in My church, and it begins in the hearts of each of My people. Be prepared to send down your roots to become firmly established in Me. Learn to hear My voice alone and obey. Don't rely on or seek others' voices or run here and there for My counsel. Sit at My feet and ask Me and I will give the knowledge and wisdom that you need. Stay close to Me, within hearing range of the Shepherd's voice and you won't wander off and be led astray. The winds and storms will come, yet those who have their roots firmly planted in Me will remain.

MUSIC SEMINAR

In late October, I learned of a praise and worship seminar coming up in November. One of my favorite worship leaders was the main instructor. I made a decision to buy plane tickets for this week-long seminar at the Montana YWAM base where Mike and I did our Discipleship Training School.

The next morning after I charged the plane tickets to Montana, I sat down with my journal and pen in hand. I heard these words in my heart:

> Let the butter of the word smooth the hardness of your heart. You have need of a cleansing, too, from harshness that would cause others to turn away from you. I have the power to change, heal, and save. Don't trust in your own ability to change. The leopard has no power to change the spots on its skin because I made it that way (Jeremiah 13:23). I made you with the nature and temperament that you have. By yourself, you have no power to change that. The joy of the Lord is your strength.

> As for money matters, stop spending. You will be in debt up to your ears. You need wisdom to bring in what you need. Look in the money envelopes designed to keep you within your means. That system was designed as a safety measure for spending. You do need limits. Make wise choices. Wait on Me before every decision and I will give you a yes or no. As for the trip to Montana, what's done is done. It is locked in place. Guilt about it is not my portion for you. Release it to Me.

"Lord, I lay this trip on the altar. Please set me free from the oppression I've carried about this trip not being from You. I've forced my way into planning this trip and Mike just went along with it."

I wanted Mike's approval, yet at the same time I felt punished. This might only have been my perception. I wanted him to hug me and melt away my sadness. I was too numb to cry.

That night, he slept on the couch, partly because he didn't want his coughing to wake me up, yet partly because of the harshness that I had displayed the night before. I slept alone.

"Lord, the anguish and torment of my guilt is overwhelming. Mike said he never wants to charge another trip. I hope that we will be able to enjoy the trip once we get there. I don't understand my own heart, and why I pushed to make this happen, or is it as my friend said, that I frantically knocked on all the doors possible.

"Lord, did You push the doors open reluctantly so I could have my own way, but You weren't in this? I want to know and to have the heaviness I feel gone. If only Mike and I were one on this once again. Forgive me for reacting in anger last night."

My child, look into My face, and let My eyes melt you.

"Lord, I can't, I've sinned."

Look into My eyes.

"Lord, I feel so guilty."

I love you, My child. I forgive you. Now, about the trip, yes, you went ahead of Me. The timing is not right. Yet I will use this trip for My glory and good will come out of it.

Relationships will be healed. The kids will bridge the gap. They will be instrumental in healing the gap between you and others. Restoring relationships is on My heart for you now.

Let Me do the work in their hearts. Stay close to Me. The timing is not yet ripe for you to step in and try to fix it with a band-aid. I'm dealing with them in a much deeper level. I know your heart is ready for reconciliation. You have reached repentance for your part in the breakdown of these relationships. Allow My Spirit to come in and melt them to the point of receiving your forgiveness. They aren't ready for it. The time will come soon for them to respond to you and you'll be ready to receive the rebuke that is coming. You already know in your heart what you've done to break the bond of friendship and violate a principle of respect for them and the knowledge they have to hear My voice. Let it go and let Me work it out.

"Okay, Lord. I see my error. I release them by an act of My will. I'm sorry for going against You with regard to the Montana trip. I give it to You. I trust You to work it out."

Now, settle down for sleep. The peace will come because now I've dealt fairly with you. My servant, you've received the instruction and correction that You've needed. Chastisement is not without a reason and the penalty will be paid.

"What do you mean, Lord?"

Learn to hear My voice more carefully. Finances will not be easy to come by. You will eventually have the money to pay for this.

"God, how did I hear so wrongly from you, and how did I think so wrongly about this trip?"

You were too wrapped up in wanting to have a break from your daily routine.

Then, God spoke to me about music, and playing piano.

Do you really seek to worship and praise Me?

"Lord, music is on my heart. I know You deserve praise and worship."

You will experience it in your heart this trip. You will see how I've created music to be played and sung back to Me. I love music, and have placed these gifts and talents in you to be used for My glory. When you glory in your own playing, the effects that your playing can have for Me are tainted.

Think of Me when you play. Thank Me for your fingers and heart for music. I will transform them to truly worship Me in Spirit and in truth. The depth of this word is hidden from you until now.

I will use your talents and gifts in music to invoke the praise and worship that are due to My name. You will lead others in worship by singing and playing to Me.

Don't focus on pleasing others. Desire to perfect those gifts for Me and not for your own glory.

These lessons will be hard to come by and not anything less than delivering a death blow to your flesh. Let Me do it once you set your mind to this. Don't think that you have reached a certain height in playing piano. Be careful, because pride comes before a fall. I long for the purity of your playing. It will come sooner than you think. Play for My enjoyment. I like to hear you play once you've set your heart in order. The hour is late. I will lead you to the rest that you need for the days ahead.

You think that brokenness is a dream you can't attain. I'm the One who breaks the clay pot and renders it useless if it becomes hard before its shape is not perfect. I need to wet it down, and start over. Get back on the potter's wheel and let Me mold you, with plenty of water so the pot becomes pliable. The potter's wheel stops, and the potter places the pot on the shelf to dry and harden in the air. A cracked and broken earthen vessel is of no value. Its pieces need to be remolded. I'll start you over. Let Me be the Potter. You be the clay. Look up the words to the song with those words. I am the Craftsman. Commit it to Me.

A few nights later, heaviness about the Montana trip, and my troubled relationship with my friend at church, kept me awake. I prayed, "Cleanse me, Lord, from all the wickedness in my heart. I went before You when I booked the plane trip to Montana after Mike finally agreed to go. Lord, You know how I wanted to escape once again to the YWAM base in Montana, the place that brought me one of the greatest joys in my life.

"Lately I have escaped in my mind when our kids were sleeping. You know I need a break from the responsibilities and stresses. Yet I cherish the joy-filled times of playing with them. I come to You for a thorough washing away the sin of selfishness."

BLIZZARD

Heavy snow began to fall on Thursday, October 31, and continued through the following day. Saturday, November 2 was our day to fly to Montana. Our neighbor called that morning at 6:20 a.m. and said, "Have you looked outside? We are in the midst of the worst blizzard in Minnesota. The snow plows have not gone by all night. The wind is howling, and the snow hasn't stopped since Thursday night. We have over 30 inches of snow! I am NOT taking you to the airport."

Mike called the airport after I talked to her. Our flight to Montana had been cancelled. There were two others today and one tomorrow. Mike decided to wait and not make any plans now. He called our neighbor back and said we could all go back to sleep.

I replied, "I can't sleep! My head is congested and I'm on the verge of a migraine headache."

Unable to sleep, I spent time with the Lord. I needed to hear from Him regarding this trip. I asked the Lord for a scripture and Acts 27:11 came to mind. The subtitle of chapter 27 in my Bible was, "WARNING AGAINST VOY-

AGE" My heart sank. "Lord, is this what You really mean about our trip?"

I read Acts 27:11 and beyond about Paul's warning the ship's pilot and crew, "Men, I can see that our voyage is going to be disastrous and bring great loss to ship and cargo, and to our own lives also. But the pilot continued on and the ship blew off course in the storm. The ship was wrecked. They landed in Malta, and after three months, Paul and the passengers safely voyaged on to Rome."

"Lord, I give up. I'm the one who put this trip together ahead of Your timing," I prayed. "I'm willing to pay for it myself with the salary from my new job at the clinic."

Later that day, during his time with the Lord, Mike also read over Paul's story in Acts 27:11. He believed that through this scripture, the Lord was guiding and warning us not to go on this trip. It was another confirmation because he sensed all along that this trip was not God's timing. Perhaps a summer trip to Montana was one we could plan instead.

There were several other confirmations after this. Our neighbor called about 1:00 p.m. and said she was not going out of the house that day. The streets had not been plowed, and the news report said that there should be no travel except for emergency vehicles. I had peace though we could be out the money if not able to use the credit for another flight. We may be out the money unless we could use the credit for another flight within a year. I fully expected to pay it all from my paycheck.

While wanting to be in Montana instead of a terribly frustrating day at home, I penned a letter to a friend about the cancelled trip,

"I am writing to you, since I trust your ability to discern my emotional state in light of my inner walk with God that you and I value in common. My anger, rage, and frustration level is extreme at this point. I don't know how to explain, except to start at the beginning of our day. First of all, our luggage is still sitting packed for our trip to YWAM Montana..."

Then, a prayer welled within, "Lord, I don't even have the energy to write why this trip to Montana didn't happen. It was much more than our flight being cancelled because of the blizzard. You warned us through Acts 27:11 that we would have been disobedient to go. Please be my Abba Father. I am so disappointed by the trip being cancelled when I looked forward to it so much."

Days later, I turned back to Acts 27:10, "Men, I can see that our voyage is going to be disastrous and bring great loss to ship and cargo, and to our own lives also." The Lord spoke these words to me:

> Trouble was awaiting you in Montana. Be glad that you did not go on the trip. Delays would have been enough for you to crack. I was protecting you from inward danger as well as outward.

> The devil roars and seeks to hurt My people. He cannot hurt but seeks to steal, rob, and destroy.

> The trip's timing was off. There will be a better time in the future. I desire to bless you as a family and for you to walk in victory for the world to see. When you are out of My will and timing, it is easier for you to lose the victory. Come under My Lordship and you will walk in victory. It is calm now. You can go back to sleep.

Next time, whenever I want to escape from my responsibilities, I'll go to the Lord instead. He may not change anything, but I will be refreshed and changed inside!

WHAT IS IN YOUR HEART?

In November, I was at a woman's retreat and a prophecy was given to the women:

My timing is not yours. I have heard the cry of your heart and I am answering My way. Trust Me with all your heart.

Through the various speakers, a theme emerged that God knows what is in our hearts.

One speaker brought up the story in Luke 8 about Jesus and the disciples in a boat when a storm arose. When the boat rocked, fear rose up in the disciples' hearts. Jesus said, "Storm, be still."

Just as the disciples became afraid in a storm, sometimes I do as well—even a storm in my heart. Jesus' words became a comfort to me that day.

Another scripture mentioned was Matthew 12:34 which says, "…out of the overflow of the heart the mouth speaks." The speaker explained that when your heart is healed, your emotions will also be healed. Above all else, guard your heart. Get rid of all bitterness and discouragement. The problem is not, "What is wrong with that person?" It is the attitude of my heart towards the other person that can get me into trouble.

I asked God to show me my heart toward certain people, and He brought particular individuals to mind. I asked His forgiveness for my attitudes toward them, and as I did, freedom flowed.

More questions were posed to dig deeper into our emotions. Another speaker said, "Ask God why you react the way you do. Ask God to search your heart. Then, sit back and watch the wonders of God's grace. It will happen in God's timing."

Three important things happened in November:

1) I started personal counseling sessions once a week, after someone helped me realize that I could benefit from professional counseling.

2) I thought I was pregnant. At that time in my life, I would have been overwhelmed to have another child, yet I accepted God's choice whatever that might be. I turned out not to be pregnant.

3) I started a clinic job on November 14. To maintain my nurse practitioner certification, I needed 1500 hours of work as a nurse practitioner in the coming five-year period. I had none. A letter came in the mail stating that my former clinic was now going to stay open on Thursday evenings from 6:00-9:00 pm. Mike and I brainstormed and prayed about me possibly working there on Thursday evenings and all day Friday when Mike could stay home with our kids. I talked to the clinic director about all of this, and he agreed to re-hire me.

"Lord, use me for Your eternal purposes," I prayed. "Build Your Kingdom through me. Light the path before me on Your righteous way. Fill my mouth with Your words of love, encouragement and comfort for my patients and co-workers."

PRAISE OF HIS GLORY RETREAT

My friend planned to speak at a retreat in December and I attended. As we sang the first song, I realized that these people from a different denomination worshipped the Lord Jesus like I did, so I relaxed. As we sang a worship song, these words came:

I'll be with you but be careful again. I led you here to be taught of Me through the speaker. Meet with her once again. Listen. Digest My words. You will be fed and nourished in your soul to face the battles at home. The inward walk is important and vital to your outward walk. You must also walk outwardly to fulfill My great commission and rub shoulders with the world. I love you and won't lead you astray.

The speaker taught about our Everlasting Father. Then she said, "God is doing some inner healing in here. He is saying these words:

I am here and I will heal you. By My Spirit I can be that Father you long for, and you can be born again as a little girl.

In my journal, I wrote, "I made mistakes with my children." God responded:

By My Spirit, your children can be restored. By My power, I cover mistakes. I am the Perfect Parent. I am not leaving you alone to raise Krista and Brian. I want you to abide in My Peace, the peace that I give you.

After the session, we could go up for prayer. As I waited for the speaker to pray for me, I wrote a short note describing my need for prayer, and gave it to her. As she prayed for me, a word from the Lord came to her for me. She had a vision. "I saw you and the Lord under a garland." He said:

You are My betrothed.

Then she said, "I also see a walnut. Your problem is not as big as you think. God can crack it and demolish it."What she believed the Lord meant was that I may see the problem as big (which had to do with my emotions), but God sees it as only the size of a walnut, easily cracked and demolished. She saw me as a soul hungering after the Lord and said, "As the deer pants for the water so my soul longs and pants after thee."

GOD'S ARMOR IN THE BATTLEFIELD

Life seemed overwhelming with two young children, ages one and one-half and three. I was often angry and frequently yelled. Conflicts with Mike seemed more intense. Krista and Brian had ear infections and Brian had a sinus infection as well. In January, I took a nursing class at a local college so I could acquire enough nurse practitioner continuing education credits for my nurse practitioner certification. All of these circumstances seemed like an intense battle.

These words came to me,

> As My word declares, Grow not weary in well doing. I will supply your needs and sustain you. I led you here by My Spirit, as I led Jesus in the wilderness for forty days to be tested and tempted by the devil. His example is one to be followed. Defeat Satan by My word. Resist him and he will flee from you. When those attacks come, pray with Mike. No weapon formed against you will prevail. Look at Ephesians 6 as an example of your armor. You are never in the battlefield alone, no matter how lonely you are. Don't isolate yourself from Mike at those times.

> As for Brian, he is sick. Take him to the doctor.

> You are almost done with this class. Lean on My grace. Do what you need to do to and study the main points for the exam.

Ephesians 6:10-19 paraphrased says, "Be strong in the Lord and in His mighty power. Put on the full armor of God so that you can take your stand against the devil's schemes. Your struggle is not against [Mike] but against the rulers, authorities, powers of this dark world and against the spiritual forces of evil in the heavenly realms. Therefore, put on the full armor from God so that when the day of evil comes [as it did on Friday night] you may be able to stand with your armor.

After you have done everything, stand with your spiritual armor on. I will train your hands for war as Psalm 18 declares. The point of attack right now is your oneness in marriage.

THE TRUTH— is to be buckled around your waist. When the attack comes, what is true in the situation? What is speculation or false perception? Ask Me for the truth and I will show you truth versus error. Ask Me together with Mike. He may not have all the truth, either, in the situation when Satan is fighting to break down your unity in marriage. Worship Me in Spirit and Truth. I am the Way, the Truth and the life.

THE RIGHTEOUSNESS— is a breastplate to protect your soul. Guard your heart with righteousness. It is right to stay married.

THE GOSPEL OF PEACE— Be ready to share the gospel, "How beautiful on the mountains are the feet of those who bring good news, who proclaim peace, who bring good tidings, who proclaim salvation, who say to Zion, 'Your God reigns!'" (Isaiah 52:7). You will not want to go into battle unless you are ready to move when I say, "Move."

FAITH— You are to hold up this shield of faith as you stand, and the fiery darts of the devil, which come as thoughts, will not penetrate your mind. Believe in Me to save you. Faith comes by hearing the word of God. Jesus is the author and finisher of your faith.

SALVATION— is to be worn as a helmet over your head and mind. You are saved. Mike is saved. You belong to Me, not Satan.

THE WORD OF GOD— is your sword of the Spirit. Use My words as a weapon in times of battle against the enemy.

PRAYER— Pray in the Spirit on all occasions. Pray in the battle with all kinds of prayers and requests.

BE ALERT—Be alert, and always pray for the saints. Pray for them in the midst of battle. Satan goes about like a roaring lion, seeking whom he can devour. Be alert to his attacks and stand firm to resist him. Be girded up so the attacks don't come near.

I prayed, "God, prepare me for battle. With You, I am ready to face the enemies of the day."

Eventually, my class ended and I passed with enough required nursing continuing education credits to renew my nurse practitioner certification. The kids took antibiotics and recovered.

WHOSE THOUGHTS?

During a prayer time at church in March, these words came to me:

Your mind is the battleground. The thoughts that you have are not your own but are of Me. As you have prayed to hear from Me, so it is. Walk in faith. They are not your burdens to carry but Mine. I am leading and guiding you in your thoughts. You have committed to bind the thoughts of the enemy from invading your mind. In Me, you have overcome, and your thoughts are My thoughts that I've placed in your mind for this time.

Isaiah 55:8 says, "For My thoughts are not your thoughts…" and that has to do with your human way of thinking. Once I place My thoughts into your mind, they transform your thoughts.

On March 23, I read Isaiah 42 & 43 and began to personalize the verses as if the Lord spoke them directly to me:

I created you, Bonnie. I formed you, and I have called you by name. You are mine. When you pass through the waters, I will be with you. When you pass through the rivers, they will not sweep over you. When you walk through the fire, you will not be burned. The flames will not set you ablaze, for I am the Lord your God, the Holy One of Israel, your Savior. Bonnie, I give Egypt for your ransom, Cush and Seba instead of you, in your place. Since you are precious and honored in My sight, Bonnie, and because I love you, I will give men in exchange for you and people in exchange for your life.

I'm going to take you out of your present church and put others in exchange for your service there. Forget the former things and do not dwell on the past.

I am doing a new thing. Now it springs up. Do you not perceive it? I am making a way in the desert. The streams will be life for you. As you enter and follow its course, I will lead you to a mighty river, a river of fellowship, with believers who run the same course as you, who are led to the mighty ocean of believers called by My name, who worship the Lamb in Spirit and in Truth. I will lead the blind by ways they have not known, along unfamiliar paths. I will guide them. I will turn the darkness into light before them and make the rough places smooth. These are the things I will do. I will not forsake them.

This is what I say in My words to you, My child. Notice the words, "I will." Yes, I will do this for you. Your chains are off. The door is open. Go. My time is soon. Fulfill your present obligations to date and then make it known to those in charge of your plans to leave.

I will lead the blind by ways they have not known. Yes, you have been blinded by untruths, and now I am allowing you to see. There is a great call on your life, and you have heard it. I have quickened it to your spirit and Mike's spirit and intend to fulfill that call. Thank you for your obedience. I will keep the vision of the great commission alive in your hearts and minds, and I intend to prepare you for the task ahead.

Then, the Lord spoke to me about other things. I received a letter from a friend and He commented about her letter:

The letter from your friend is timely. It is to encourage and steady you. Drink in the words of life that I am giving through her. This is a time for refreshing, restoring, and strengthening. These moments in silence are well taken while your children sleep. Soak in the rays of My sunshine. My Son shines on you and in you as you change to become His bride. You are mighty and a great part of My Bride.

I am preparing you through the lessons with Mike, the children, and relationships with people at church. Others are being tested in trials I especially designed for them by Me. As the trials and tests come, stay close to Me You are not alone in these experiences.

As you are in this learning process, you need not be afraid of failure. Even if you occasionally fail or choose less than My perfect ways for you in daily life, I will be there to encourage and strengthen you. Learn a lesson from the apostle Peter. I said to him, "Simon, Simon, Satan has asked to sift you as wheat. But I have prayed for you, Simon, that your faith may not fail. And when you turn back, strengthen your brothers" (Luke 22:31). I knew Peter more than he knew himself. He thought he'd never deny Me, yet I knew he would. I prayed for him and allowed Satan to sift him. Peter denied Me three times, but just as I said he would, when Peter turned back, he did strengthen his brothers and became a mighty leader and pillar in the church.

I can do the same for you when you fail. I love you, and won't leave or forsake you in times of failure. I know your heart means well, yet you set yourself up to fail if you expect perfection when you don't reach the straight and narrow one hundred percent of the time. This thinking comes from trying to measure up to an expectation you set without receiving My grace. I don't expect perfection from you. The more you hear My voice and obey, the more you will walk along the straight and narrow path. I will protect you from danger and the enemy's prowl. You are in My hand, and you will be protected with the armor as you put it on. Don't hesitate to call on Me, and I will send angel messengers to protect you from stumbling.

Think of the narrow path in Banaue, Philippines. The path was easy at first. It climbed up the mountain and went along rice paddy terraces, where a fall to the left would leave you in parasite-infested waters and a fall to the right would cause you to fall off the mountain. As you heard, "Look straight ahead, neither to the right or to the left," and as your feet clung to the narrow terrace path, you were safe. I kept you from falling by your obedience to me. That's how it works in this journey of faith and in the kingdom life. Your fears of failure as you try to measure up to Me are based on false expectations that you have for yourself. I don't expect you to measure up to My standards on your own.

Walk in the light of what you know. Obey Me, and I am pleased. I am disappointed when you fail, yet I don't love you any less. Be released to fail and not measure up. Let Me be in charge of your journey on this walk. I lead; you follow. You are not alone. I go before you on the narrow path. Think of Me going before you on the rice paddy terrace. You could trust Me then. Trust Me now and hear My still, small voice. Turn to Isaiah 30:21, "Whether you turn to the right or to the left, your ears will hear a voice behind you saying, 'This is the way; walk in it.'"

Don't be anxious about where you will go to church. My time to move you on is near. It will happen so naturally that you won't think it is supernatural. My way of peace will be a hallmark stamp with no mistaking it. Go in the direction your heart is leading you. There will be tension, and there will be those who don't understand, but don't let that keep you from following your heart after Me. I will be merciful and kind. My grace will be sufficient for them to accept your leaving. In time, the hurt they may feel when you leave will cease, and I will heal them as I bring those to take your place.

Don't forget Isaiah 43:4, "Since you are precious and honored in my sight, and because I love you, I will give men in exchange for you, and people in exchange for your life."

I am doing a major rearranging of My people. I know where best to transplant them.

At the end of March, God spoke these words:

Rest and quietness is your portion today, allowing you and your family to heal. Staying tuned to My Holy Spirit's voice will be important to keep your heart at rest and your mind in perfect peace. I will close doors before you if you try to move around to get more things accomplished.

You are in need of rest. Don't be concerned if everything in the natural seems to be standing still. I am at work and am moving by My Spirit.

Learn a lesson from the tiny sprouts beneath the ground. To the farmer looking on, the ground has not broken with new life, yet the seed has germinated and the sprout is finding its way to the surface. Growth happens in the dark, and long before fruit is born. Patience and long suffering is needed, as well as provision of water and fertilizer for growth. Sunshine comes after the sprout has broken through the bare ground.

Work diligently. Plod along. Growth will happen.

GOD'S CHURCH

One evening, Mike and I attended a meeting at the Minneapolis Christ Center in the old Camden Theatre where YWAM's founder was speaking. As he shared, it was awesome to catch a glimpse of what God was doing in His worldwide church. As I pondered what he said, these words came to me the next morning:

> *My church is reaching out in My time, My way, first to neighbors, the city, the country, then to the outermost parts of the world. Keep your vision alive. My church is not programs, marketing, surveys, or practices. It is about people and spreading the gospel. Numbers don't matter. Be led by My Spirit, not by practices. Keep My vision alive.*

In April, I sensed that our church was in a dark place of oppression, although I didn't know of any problem.

On a Sunday, one of the apostolic overseers of our church delivered the sermon. While he spoke, these words came to me:

> *Get out of the cave and you'll ask different questions. I'll bring you into a different place. If you are in a dark place, you will lose your sensitivity to your work and sensitivity to others.*

When I was in the Philippines, the Lord had said to me:

> *Don't touch the Lord's anointed.*

Again, God wanted me to search my heart concerning the pastor and church. Whether we stayed at this church or moved on, I knew my attitude needed to be right toward the pastor and others. "Thank You, Lord that You care and know what is happening."

I grieved because of limited fellowship at our present church. God said,

You have been deprived of fellowship. Yet, it is not your place to say, "This one should go, or that one should stay."

There is a deep work going on in every church. Once others reach a place of discontentment and putting their roots down deep in Me, and not just in the church, then it becomes easier for Me to transplant them.

My church is a church on the move, willing and ready to go when and where I call them for service and for battle. My church is without walls. It is a place where fellowship with one another thrives. Read in Joel about My army. My church is made up of servants, laying down their lives, soldiers with their faces to the cross for the joy set before them.

The army of the Lord described in Joel 2 is a large, mighty army. Nothing escapes them. They charge like warriors. They scale walls like soldiers. They all march in line, not swerving from their course. They do not jostle each other. Each marches straight ahead. They plunge through defenses without breaking ranks, rush upon the city, run along the wall, climb into houses, and enter through the window. The earth shakes before them.

The Lord thunders at the head of the army. His forces are beyond number, and mighty are those who obey His command.

Do not seek a place of refuge where you would only obtain spiritual food. You may be in a season for that, but trust Me to lead you there and it won't be by your own striving. My kingdom is not one where complacency reigns. Don't get too settled in the comfort of one place. Only get settled and strengthened in Me as I give you spiritual food, drink, fellowship, and rest.

Be ready to move on at a moment's notice. My place for you is in Me. As you move, live, have your being and identi-

ty in Me, and you will thrive and bubble over with joy in the places where I send you. Your eyes will be on Me to please Me, and to take pleasure, satisfaction, and joy from Me. Arise, shine, for your Light has come. I am your Light to lead the way out of darkness until there is no more darkness left, only bright shining light.

Have a good day.

At the end of April, I prayed, "Lord, lead and guide this time of fellowship and communion with You." These words came to mind:

Learn a lesson from the fig tree. Its roots go deep. It bears fruit when the conditions are right. The fruit needs to ripen first before it is edible. The tree cannot say to its gardener, "I want more fruit." It needs sunshine, rain, and pruning before the fruit will appear. Bad fruit comes only if it falls from the tree and rots.

The fruit of the Spirit, especially of patience and longsuffering that comes in circumstances such as yours, are gems. They are instilling My character in you. Ask for sunshine, rain, and the pruning away of everything that is not of Me. I will cause the fruit of patience and longsuffering to come. Others will see it and wonder. Don't take credit for what I do. It is only as My Spirit works in you that the fruit of longsuffering and patience will come for all to see.

Set your face like flint to the test. You will not break under the pressures and the heat of the crucible. The dross will come to the surface. You will be tried in the fire until nothing is left but Me. Don't worry if you don't see the fruit now. Wait for My timing. Let Me work in you during the present trials and those to come.

I am amazed at how many trials came my way during that time. Brian turned two years old and was very active. My job as a nurse practitioner was a huge challenge. I cried out to the Lord during my suffering. God's word that day became truth.

CALM WORD TO A TROUBLED MIND

I asked the Lord to be a refuge from my stormy mind. He spoke to my heart:

Rest, My child. Your mind is troubled with many things. Seek My face. You shall live with abundant life. The "pressure cooker" experiences of your life will soon be turned off, and your dross will come to the surface to be skimmed off by Me. No amount of your stirring and stewing inside will take care of it, so rest. The time of completion of this trial is coming to a close. I see the end from the beginning and it will be soon. Don't fret.

Proverbs 14:30 says, "A heart at peace gives life to the body…"

During another prayer time, the Lord said:

Today I want you to rejoice and be glad as I have mighty plans for you to shape the lives of your children. Love them, care for them, correct them, and sow seeds of righteousness. The day is short. You'll get the rest you need because I know you are tired and have to rest.

Today will not be a hard day. Be obedient to Me regarding what to say. I have mighty plans for you to give you hope. It will be a fresh start. Arise, shine. Jesus is your Light today, outside and within you.

In May, I met with a Christian counselor to help me with my anger issues. One day the Lord spoke to me about my counselor:

I am working through your counselor. You need to weed out the things that are not from Me, but I will give you wisdom to know what is of Me and what is of the world's philosophy. I have given her wisdom and insight from years of experience and counsel. Rest in Me, knowing that I will guide

*you to emotional health. This is the way and path I have cho-
sen for you.*

UNFULFILLED DREAMS

In June, I poured my heart out in prayer, "Lord, so many dreams of mine have gone by the wayside. I wanted to travel to Montana, but the trip fell through. I wanted to attend my cousin's wedding in Hawaii; however, another cousin's son's wedding came up on the same day, and I sensed that I should attend that wedding instead. I wanted to make a trip to Montana for a YWAM summer camp, but it was too expensive. "Lord, why did these unfulfilled dreams happen?" I heard the Lord say,

The key to all of these things is that you need to be in My place for you at any given time. My workings in your family are crucial right now. Your time with them is shorter than you realize. Planting seeds of faith in them this past weekend was crucial.

I replied, "Jesus, I don't want to be guided by my emotions or way of understanding. I ask that You would help me to discern Your voice."

You were not led and guided by My peace. You did not have one-hundred percent peace in buying that ticket for the Montana trip. Your family needs to be together right now. This is an important key for your children's foundational lives. The time will come when they can be more independent of you. They need your influence. You and Mike need to be alone at times, more than ever, and I'll lead you. Cling close to Me and I won't disappoint you by waiting.

One night I had a dream one night about a vine that came up the stairs of my paternal grandfather's house. In the dream, I tried to warn people that the vine was coming to invade them. In the morning, I asked the Lord what scripture to read. The scripture Psalm 78:8 came to mind, "They would not be like their ancestors—a stubborn and rebellious generation, whose hearts were not loyal to God, whose spirits were not faithful to Him." None of this made sense. The next day, these words came to me:

Be not fearful or dismayed by My teaching about spiritual strongholds and roots of your fathers. I will be one to set you free of it all, so you can worship Me and do My will.

ABOUT THE BOOK

On October 12, 1992, Mike and I visited another church to hear its former pastors whom we knew. During the sermon, I wrote these words about the book I believe I was to write:

"Now what?" you may say. No, this is not the end of My words to you, but the end of this book. I will begin a new chapter in your life.

Writing down My word is of Me. It is for you and others who long to know that I am a personal God. I am One Who speaks. Come to Me and I will touch your heart. I will touch your tongue with a burning coal to begin speaking the word of the Lord to others to encourage, edify, and to build them up.

Wait on Me, for I will surely bring My words to pass. I will write them on the tablets of your heart.

A NOTE FROM THE AUTHOR

This was indeed just the beginning of a series of "new books" the Lord wrote on my heart starting in 1981. The words in this first book have been foundational for me. They have guided me through change and deep healing, and they tell the story of my growing trust in the Lord.

My prayer is that if you found any words that touched you in this book, they will lead you into that same trusting relationship the Lord has for all His children, the sheep of His pasture.